PE

RI

Laura Ashe is Associate Professor of English and a Fellow of Worcester College, Oxford. Her books include *Fiction and History in England, 1066–1200* and the *Oxford English Literary History, vol. 1: 1000–1350. Conquest and Transformation.* She has also edited *Early Fiction in England: From Geoffrey of Monmouth to Chaucer* for Penguin Classics. The extraordinary flowering of English literature in the reign of Richard II features in much of her work.

LAURA ASHE

Richard II

A Brittle Glory

PENGUIN BOOKS

PENGUIN BOOKS

UK | USA | Canada | Ireland | Australia
India | New Zealand | South Africa

Penguin Books is part of the Penguin Random House group of companies whose addresses can be found at global.penguinrandomhouse.com.

First published by Allen Lane 2016
First published in Penguin Books 2018
001

Set in 9.5/13.5 pt Sabon LT Std
Typeset by Jouve (UK), Milton Keynes
Printed and bound in Great Britain by Clays Ltd, Elcograf S.p.A.

ISBN: 978–0–141–98736–1

www.greenpenguin.co.uk

Penguin Random House is committed to a sustainable future for our business, our readers and our planet. This book is made from Forest Stewardship Council® certified paper.

Contents

Prologue

. . . O flattering glass,
Like to my followers in prosperity,
Thou dost beguile me! Was this face the face
That every day under his household roof
Did keep ten thousand men? Was this the face
That like the sun did make beholders wink?
Is this the face which faced so many follies,
That was at last outfaced by Bolingbroke?
A brittle glory shineth in this face.
As brittle as the glory is the face,
For there it is, cracked in a hundred shivers.

Shakespeare, *Richard II*[1]

In the act of resigning his crown to Bolingbroke, the future Henry IV, Shakespeare's Richard asks for a mirror, and stares disbelievingly at his unchanged face. This is a king who has been sustained by a vision, the image of his own glorious kingship. Now unkinged, he cannot make sense of his own face in the mirror; he smashes the glass, and shatters the image. A king is not dismantled from within, as a man's character may be broken down by circumstance. A king has no interior; his whole existence lies in his face, his crown, his glory.

Shakespeare's Richard is an amalgam of the chronicle

sources, turned to the playwright's dramatic purposes. The play opens in 1397, with a high-handed and immature king; the path to his deposition is inexorable, and his folly and Bolingbroke's usurpation sow the bloody seeds of the Wars of the Roses, which tore England apart in the fifteenth century. History itself knows no such necessities. King Richard II of England was crowned at the age of ten in July 1377, and deposed twenty-two years later, on 30 September 1399. He lived for a few months more, in close imprisonment, and died in February 1400. Contemporary accounts give several different versions of Richard's death – that he was cruelly starved, that he starved himself out of despair, that he heroically fought off an assassination party of several attackers before being struck from behind – and chroniclers observe that many believed he still lived. Henry IV displayed Richard's corpse to the public, his face uncovered, in an attempt to convince the populace of his identity and prevent any further attempts to restore him to the throne. In death as in life, Richard was an image offered up for recognition.

Richard's face, as he wished it to be seen, is well known to us. He made two great artistic commissions around 1395: the Westminster Abbey portrait, in which he faces us enthroned with crown, orb and sceptre; and the Wilton Diptych altarpiece, where he kneels before the Virgin Mary and Christ Child with a choir of angels, supported by the blessing of the saints King Edmund the Martyr, King Edward the Confessor and John the Baptist. Both images depict a youthful, beardless face; smooth, pale skin and fair hair, with a small mouth and delicately shaped nose. Richard's decision at the age of twenty-eight to present himself so boyishly has occasioned some perplexity among historians. But perhaps this was the idealized light in which he saw himself throughout his life.

He had been crowned and anointed as a child, at the culmination of an astonishing display of pageantry and festivity in London, heralded by hundreds of trumpeters and the cheers of thousands, when the fountains ran with wine and beautiful maidens cast golden coins at his feet.[2] Richard conceived of kingship as an essential part of his identity; at the very end he declared himself incapable of casting off the spiritual character with which he had been imprinted at his anointing.[3] He would not do it, he said, and angrily added that he would very much like to know *how* a king can resign a crown, and to whom.[4] 'Not all the water in the rough rude sea / Can wash the balm off from an anointed king';[5] Shakepeare's ventriloquy of Richard captures an unshakeable faith in the divine qualities of kingship, and in the transformative and indelible nature of the ceremony by which the young prince was made a king. One chronicle tells a famous story which has stuck, despite being otherwise unattested, because it seems to encapsulate Richard's hauteur, and also his loneliness. We are told that at the height of his power he had a throne made for his chamber, 'wherein he was wont to sit after dinner until the hour of evensong, speaking to no man, but overlooking all men; and if he looked upon any man, whatever his estate or degree, that man must kneel'.[6]

Richard had not been expected to inherit the throne so young. His father, Edward, the 'Black Prince' of Wales

(1330–76), embodied the chivalry of the age, and led England to great military victories in France in the first decades of the Hundred Years War. Admired by English and French alike, he was celebrated as a heroic figure and protector of the English nation. With his early death, one chronicler extravagantly declared, the hopes of the English died too.[7] The elderly Edward III expired amid some political chaos the following year, and ten-year-old Richard came to the throne as a fragile but optimistic promise of peace and accord, supported by a great council established for his minority, with the agreement of the Commons and the Lords. In Parliament the Archbishop of Canterbury insisted that 'although the very noble and powerful prince my lord Edward, recently Prince of Wales, was departed and called to God, nevertheless the prince was as if present and not in any way absent, because he had left behind him such a noble and fine son, who is his exact image or true likeness'.[8]

This may have been the first public use of Richard's face and body as the epitome of kingship, but it was very wide of the mark; he would never be a martial figure like his father. He pursued a different ideal: kings had always balanced military might with a sacred duty to the maintenance of peace and justice in the realm, and it was this latter vision which gave purpose to his rule, and – ironically – brought about his downfall. Richard's difficulties were many, but the essence of his personal failings seems to have lain in the confluence of these two great ideas – the divinity of kingship and the perfection of peace – because for Richard, 'peace' in the sense that he valued it meant the complete obedience of every subject to the will of the king.

The Westminster portrait makes it easy to believe that where this man's gaze fell, the subject should kneel. His face is calm and inscrutable, dwarfed by the signs of his office and status. This is no Henry VIII to command obedience by sheer force of personality; rather, Richard's image enacts kingship itself, around a curious void. As an individual, he is absent from the portrait; as king, he is presented for our veneration. In contrast, the Wilton Diptych shows Richard in a posture of supplication, either offering or receiving some gift. But his supplication is to heaven, to the Virgin and Christ Child; his gaze is fixed in prayer, away from us. Once again, the viewer is made to recognize the sheer glory of kingship, its otherworldly status, and Richard's distance from his subjects. This majesty is revealed by the actual events of Richard's life and death to have been empty at its heart. One English chronicler placed such an accusation into Richard's own mouth: 'And then King Richard confessed how he had greatly trespassed against God and the realm, and that he was not worthy to reign, for he knew well, he said, that he loved never the people, nor the people him.'[9] Shakespeare captured the Richard whose whole identity was the glory of kingship; this anonymous chronicler casts him as an individual who failed to provide the heart and soul which were supposed to live beneath the image.

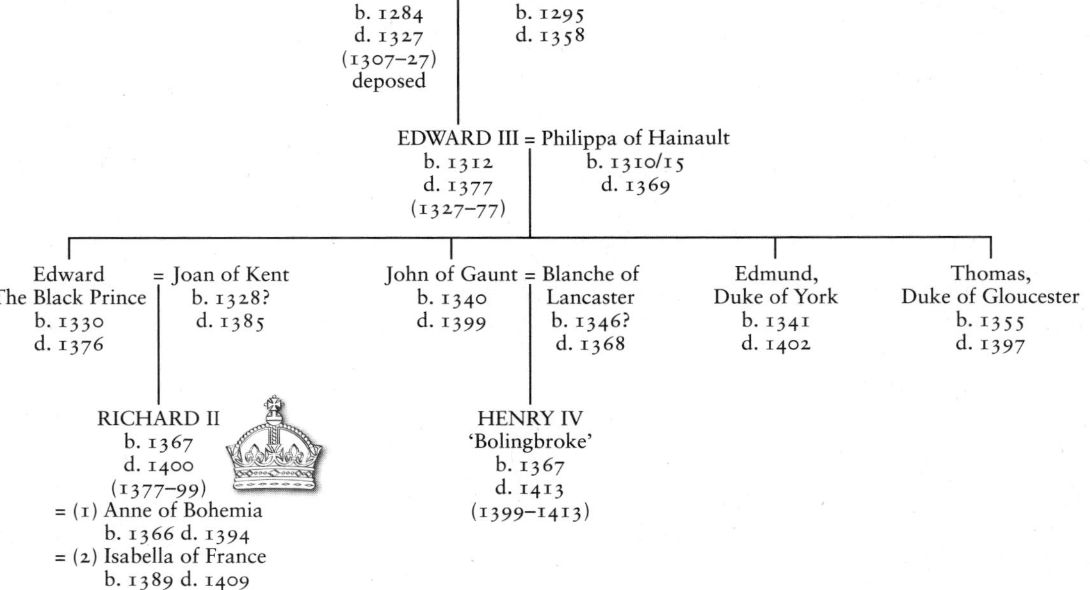
EDWARD II = Isabella of France
b. 1284
d. 1327
(1307–27)
deposed
b. 1295
d. 1358
EDWARD III = Philippa of Hainault
b. 1312
d. 1377
(1327–77)
b. 1310/15
d. 1369
Edward
The Black Prince
b. 1330
d. 1376
= Joan of Kent
b. 1328?
d. 1385
John of Gaunt = Blanche of Lancaster
b. 1340
d. 1399
b. 1346?
d. 1368
Edmund,
Duke of York
b. 1341
d. 1402
Thomas,
Duke of Gloucester
b. 1355
d. 1397
RICHARD II
b. 1367
d. 1400
(1377–99)
= (1) Anne of Bohemia
b. 1366 d. 1394
= (2) Isabella of France
b. 1389 d. 1409
HENRY IV
'Bolingbroke'
b. 1367
d. 1413
(1399–1413)

Richard II

I
Parliament

> Must I do so? and must I ravel out
> My weaved-up follies?[1]

> The question of deposing King Richard and replacing him as king with Henry duke of Lancaster, and of how and for what reasons this might lawfully be done, was committed for debate to a number of doctors, bishops and others, one of whom was the writer of this present work; and they decided that perjuries, sacrileges, sodomitical acts, dispossession of his subjects, the reduction of his people to servitude, lack of reason, and incapacity to rule, to all of which King Richard was notoriously prone, were sufficient reasons . . . for deposing him. Moreover, although he was prepared to abdicate, it was nevertheless decided that, as a further precaution, he should be deposed by the authority of the clergy and people.[2]

The author of this eyewitness account was a lawyer named Adam Usk, who began writing his chronicle in 1401. The decision to depose Richard had been taken long before the official reasons for it could be satisfactorily shaped, as Usk unapologetically reveals. In legal terms the situation was extremely delicate; the best precedent they had was the deposition of the emperor Frederick II by Pope Innocent IV in 1245, but the pope's authority over a king was of a fundamentally different order from that of a king's own subjects over him. In English experience, similar crises had had different outcomes: in 1216 John had fortunately died at a moment when the rebellious magnates could transfer their support to the young Henry III; Simon de Montfort's death at Evesham in 1265 had ended real rebellion during Henry's long reign, and his son Edward I became the first king after the Conquest to succeed unopposed. The removal of Edward II in 1327 had been softened by his son and heir's immediate accession as Edward III (albeit under the control of others). Richard had no heir of his body, and he was young and in good health; he would have to be destroyed. The historical parallels did not escape him. When Usk visited the imprisoned king in the Tower and saw him at dinner, Richard declared bitterly that 'this is a strange and fickle land, which has exiled, slain, destroyed, and ruined so many kings', then 'recounted the names and the histories of those who had suffered such fates'.[3]

Usk's chronicle reveals the strains involved in this newly minted legal process. He describes a lengthy argument which attempted simply to put Richard out of the line of succession, by means of a rumour that Edward I was not in fact the firstborn son of Henry III – which Usk himself disproves by citation of numerous chronicles and records. He further records a more scurrilous rumour that Richard himself was the result of his mother's adultery, and therefore illegitimate. Neither allegation was pursued. The list of crimes with which Richard was eventually charged is so exhaustive as to be meaningless. The reasons for Richard's deposition were essentially personal, in a manner which collides painfully both with the codification of a king's deposition in law, and with the abstract divinity of kingship which he had spent his life trying to embody. As the chroniclers present us with their different visions of Richard, we can see that the true battleground of his reign was the king's image, the face he presented, and its interpretation by those around him. The story in this book is told largely through the accounts of eyewitnesses, and contemporary chroniclers, because it is the story of how Richard was perceived.[4]

The book is arranged by four locations, each both real and imagined: parliament, battlefield, city, shrine. There is an obvious omission – the court. This was a decision which came about in the process of writing, for considering the court in the context of these other locations highlights the paradoxes which surround Richard. The court was not after all a place: it was a collection of people around the king, and it was an idea. Where the king travelled, the physical court travelled with him: the noblemen and ladies in attendance on the king and queen (these were the only 'courtiers'), with their own attendants and servants, their packhorses and carts of provisions and luxuries; the musicians and performers, men-at-arms and their horses, cooks and chambermaids, seamstresses, embroiderers and furriers, scribes and administrators; and all the petitioners, those seeking employment or preferment, the hangers-on. In royal manor houses they could rapidly install the king's household to an appropriate level of luxury; in abbeys and towns on the road, hundreds of them might be camped out while the king and queen made do with the best accommodation that could be vacated for them. The expense to their hosts was often punitively high.

The idea of the court was more important than these logistics, and more difficult to control. Richard invested in majesty, in the display of dazzling wealth and intricate ceremony; but if his subjects were to believe in the court as he wished, as a demonstration of glorious kingship, they would have to see some substance of power and regality within the show. Richard encountered particular difficulties in this. The king's court was supposedly the true centre of power in the realm, and his grandfather had nurtured this image. Edward III's court had been a celebration of England's chivalrous knighthood and success in war, led by the king as a new King Arthur, host to the Order of the Garter. But when the ten-year-old Richard was crowned, power resided with the council appointed for his minority, with the greatest magnates, and with Parliament. As the war with France lapsed into a series of truces, the court ceased to be a gathering of the flower of chivalry; men with martial ambitions had to look elsewhere. One chronicler sneered that the court was full of knights who were more valiant in bed than on the battlefield; observers commented on the presence of numerous women, whom they thought 'useless' and an expense for the royal household to support.[5]

Richard's court was necessarily no more than a forum for display while he was a child; yet as he grew older, his taste for the performance of ceremony, deference and largesse only increased. Some of his sense of his proper dignity can be gleaned from the praise poem written by Richard Maidstone in 1392, commemorating Richard II's ceremonial procession into London. The poem could possibly have been a commission; it certainly sought to represent the king as he would wish himself to be seen. Richard's beauty is compared with that of Troilus and Absalom, and he is greeted by the Londoners seeking his favour with dramatized obeisance:

> The king pulls back the golden reins and halts his steed;
> At this the people and the nobles all fall still.
> The warden then draws near, with aldermen in robes;
> His left hand holds the keys, his right hand holds a sword,
> Its point toward himself . . .
> 'Your majesty, whose awful power is to be feared
> And also to be loved, and equally revered,
> Behold: your humble citizens, beneath your feet
> Surrender all they have and their own selves to you.
> With keys and sword the city gives up willingly:
> It comes all ready to surrender to your will.'

After a long procession through the decorated streets, the king comes at last to his throne in the palace of Westminster:

> The decoration of the hall and its array
> Would be no easy task to tell or to unfold.
> The house was overspread with all the weaver's skill;
> The gaze was stunned at such an unaccustomed sight.

The royal throne has pride of place upon the dais,
Bedecked with coverings of nothing but fine gold.
The scepter-wielding king then mounts the gleaming throne;
The nobles stand there, urging silence on the crowd.[6]

The repeated image is of vast crowds cheering in adulation and then stilled by the sheer beauty and charisma of the king; he is beyond them all in glory, appropriately surrounded by the superabundant offering of gold, jewels, banqueting tables, tapestries, music. The scene is dazzling, and we are instructed to be dazzled.

Towards the height of his power, in October 1396, Richard held a conference over several days with Charles VI of France, to ratify the terms of Richard's marriage agreement with the seven-year-old Princess Isabella. The festivities were wildly expensive to arrange, and to crown their ritual of friendship the two kings presented one another with gifts of increasing value. Richard produced a buckle worth more than £300 and a goblet and pitcher worth £200; later he presented another huge golden cup and pitcher worth £470, and finally he seems to have won the competition with a necklace of pearls and precious stones which had belonged to his first queen, said to be worth as much as £3,300.[7] These figures are difficult to translate into modern monetary terms, but certainly amount to an impressive fortune.[8] More inventively (though the English chronicler who is the source of our account did not know their value), Charles presented Richard with a goblet and pitcher filled with pearls and jewels, and a model ship in gold, mounted at either end with the figure of a tiger looking in a mirror. Richard wore a different, fabulously expensive gown each day of the conference (while poor Charles only had one outfit). On the day that Richard wore a long red velvet gown and a hat covered with pearls, the two rulers 'spoke together for a long time, and at their meeting all the people of the one side and the other knelt for a long time on the ground'. Eventually, the writer says, 'for the comfort of the people' the kings rose, and walked hand in hand to admire first the French then the English knights drawn up in their finest array, before withdrawing to Charles's pavilion for further gift-giving.[9]

Such performances were an indispensable part of the intricate dance of international diplomacy; a king had to assert his magnificence and munificence among his only peers. But at home, despite Richard's hopes for the respect and submission of his people, from the earliest years of his attempted self-governance his actions brought him into conflict with the other powers in the realm. Chroniclers had long observed Richard's 'lust for glory and his eagerness to have from everybody the deference properly due to kingship'.[10] As a young king he had sought to purchase both glory and deference with extreme largesse, which became a continual source of rancour in Parliament, as the chroniclers relate:

> In his early years this king of ours was so open-handed that to make any legitimate request of him was to have it immediately granted; indeed at times he anticipated the wishes of petitioners and he used often to give more than had been asked for. So lavish was his bounty, however, that all the

> property attaching to the Crown, in common with the revenues belonging to the royal exchequer, was virtually dealt out piecemeal to various people who presented demands for this or that.[11]

This was a substantial accusation, with important legal implications. On the one hand, the king could use the income from crown property as he wished, to fund his household and court, but such royal property should not be alienated from the crown, to the impoverishment of his own estate and that of his heirs. The revenues of the royal exchequer were another matter altogether: they were to be used for the good of the kingdom. This had long been a vague distinction, for the king's own expenses when at war or engaged in diplomacy might appropriately come from the public purse, but Richard's profligacy made it an urgent question. In particular both the Commons and the Lords were enraged by the sense that corrupt favourites were using the young king for their own ends, growing rich themselves while he, 'having thus handed out his own substance to others . . . had perforce to come down on the commons, with the result that the poor are loud in their complaints and declare that they cannot go on supporting the burden'.[12] These accusations were to wax and wane in strength throughout his reign, periodically bringing it to crisis. Writing after the king's fall, one chronicler repeated a rumour that Richard had ordered a robe to be made for him 'of gold and pearls and other precious stones', supposedly worth the unimaginable sum of £20,000.[13] Richard had become a symbol of outrageous pride and extravagance.

The idea of the court sustained Richard, and he sustained it, at vast expense. He surrounded himself with courtiers who stood to gain from his largesse, and who therefore flattered and praised him as he wished. He experienced his court – his day-to-day life of hunting, or feasting, or games – as the place where the king's will was enacted without question, and he believed that this was as it should be. But beyond his court circle all was very different, in ways which Richard seems not to have understood. There were three important spheres of power which overlapped with the court, but maintained independence from it, and from the king's will. First, his greatest magnates: they expected to exercise their customary role of advising and helping to direct international and domestic policy. For Richard this amounted to their coming to him with tiresome and unwelcome instruction and admonishment – his uncles demanding war with France, bishops protesting the rights of the Church to lands held by the crown. Second, his councillors, the chief officers of the realm; in the early years such men were appointed by Parliament and not by the king. Richard experienced the execution of their duties as a series of attempts to block his desires, to which he responded with rage – in 1382 he removed his chancellor for refusing to ratify charters giving away great landholdings; the 'ambitious men' who stood to gain had persuaded the king that, by denying them, the chancellor showed 'contempt for the royal command'.[14] And finally, above all, Richard faced Parliament, the great machine of government of the realm, which could cut off his income by refusing to grant levies of taxation, and always insisted on examining the reasons for his requests. Richard understood his own reign through the distorting lens of the court he made for himself; he could not understand why the regality he regarded as his right was denied to him on the broader stage.

The court is not a focus of this book, therefore, despite its centrality to Richard's imagination of himself. From this distance, Richard's reign is better explained as a series of parliaments, violent struggles for power played out in ponderous legal prose over weeks of circular discussion, and periodically in blood on the executioner's block. The parliaments of this period constituted an intricate legal framework for the channelling of individuals' desires into power over the whole kingdom. The essence of the question was simple: who could manipulate Parliament for his own ends most successfully without openly destroying it?

In the so-called 'Wonderful Parliament' of 1386, when Richard was nineteen years old, his wealthy favourites were impeached and his chancellor, Michael de la Pole, condemned for treason and imprisoned. Richard attempted to halt proceedings by withdrawing from Westminster to Eltham while Parliament was in session; the Lords and Commons sent messages to the king stating that his chancellor and treasurer should both be removed from office, and Richard famously responded that he would not dismiss so much as a kitchen boy on their orders.[15] At this, the Duke of Gloucester and Thomas Arundel, Bishop of Ely, came to see the king, and told him that ancient statute required him to hold Parliament once a year, where 'the errors of the kingdom can be corrected, and the state and governance of the king and the kingdom considered with the wisest counsel', not least, they added pointedly, because 'as [the people] bear the burden they should also oversee in what manner and by whom their goods and chattels are expended'.[16]

Richard reportedly then threatened to ask the King of France for help against his rebellious subjects, which Gloucester and Arundel dismissed contemptuously, noting the 'endless exertions' and 'tireless endeavour' of Richard's father and grandfather to conquer that great enemy. Finally, they cited an 'ancient statute' held by the people of England, 'which not long since, lamentably, had to be invoked', by which a king who would 'estrange himself from his people, and will not be governed and guided by the laws of the land . . . and the wholesome counsel of the lords and nobles of the kingdom, but wrong-headedly, upon his own unsound conclusions, follows the promptings of his untempered will' might 'with the common assent and agreement of the people of the realm' lawfully be deposed.[17] No such statute existed, but the memory of his great-grandfather Edward II's deposition certainly did, and Richard capitulated. In late October he returned to Parliament to ratify the removal of his favourites.

The Lords' and Commons' motivation for action was openly stated: 'that by the greed of the king's ministers the goods of the kingdom were all but consumed to no good effect, the king greatly deceived, and the people of the kingdom impoverished by heavy burdens ... and that amidst all these things the king's officials were beyond measure grown rich'.[18] Beside the chancellor, de la Pole, these 'officials' included Robert de Vere, whom Richard had stubbornly promoted to the great title of Duke of Ireland on 13 October, sparking the immediate crisis; and Nicholas Brembre, several times Mayor of London, whom Richard had supported for years. In an astonishing gesture of authority over the king, Parliament set up a commission of lords of the realm who would 'take over the management of all matters', effectively rendering Richard powerless. The Commons pleaded 'that the said lords and officers may be able to correct and amend all the faults through which your crown is so harmed, as well because the laws and statutes are not at all upheld and protected, as because other goods and profits whatsoever are withdrawn from your said crown'.[19] The chronicler adds that the Lords sought to gain Richard's 'greater benevolence and favour' for the arrangement by granting him an extra round of taxation income, but only 'if it should seem necessary to the aforesaid councillors'.[20]

These constraints were untenable to Richard, who promptly released his chancellor from prison and set off on a progress around the country, apparently to avoid the lord commissioners while he decided on his next move. He summoned the sheriffs from the counties and told them to prepare to muster forces to fight against the lords who opposed him, and to agree that they would not return any knight to Parliament whom the king had not chosen; both demands, the one amounting to civil war, the other to the corruption of Parliament, were refused.[21]

In August 1387, Richard called a panel of judges to attend him at Shrewsbury, where he and his favourites asked them to pronounce on whether the measures of the 1386 parliament had been lawful. They answered that they had not been: since the king had been 'coerced', he 'could annul and change such ordinances at his pleasure . . . because he was not subject to those laws'.[22] In Nottingham on 25 August, Richard then gathered all the judges of the realm – though one lucky Sir William Skipworth did not attend because of illness – and forced them to fix their seals to a statement that 'the new statute and ordinance and commission made in the last parliament held at Westminster were derogatory to the regality and prerogative of our said lord the king', and that those who had 'procured the aforesaid statute . . . deserved to suffer the capital punishment, namely of death, unless the king wished to grant them his grace therein'.[23] One judge, Robert Bealknap, famously refused to comply until threatened with death on the spot – and miserably commented that he had only delayed the inevitable, for 'because I have done the king's will . . . I shall be judged to a traitor's death by the lords of the realm'.[24] He was indeed condemned with all the others in the next parliament, but the sentence was mercifully commuted to exile in Ireland.[25]

Richard returned to London to a great welcome from the citizens, decked in the king's colours of red and white, and he must have hoped that this show of support indicated a turn in his favour.[26] But when he asked the Londoners to fight for him, they refused. Richard's cause was impossibly unpopular. It is hard to imagine many people in 1387 believing that it was truly in the king's interests to fight for the 'Duke of Ireland' de Vere, the wealthy and corrupt de la Pole, and their associates. Richard's insistent support of his favourites demonstrated too well that he followed his singular will rather than justice and truth:

> It is said that Ralph, Lord Basset, said to the king, 'My lord, you know that I have been, am, and ever shall be your faithful liegeman, and my body and all I possess are and will be subject to your justice and truth, but I must tell you that if I have to go into battle, I wish unmistakably to be with the party that is true and seeks the truth, and that I am not going to offer to have my head broken for the duke of Ireland.'[27]

De Vere raised an army from Cheshire and the Welsh borders, and marched towards London in an attempt to reach Richard. He was cut off by the lords and their (much greater) forces in Oxfordshire on 20 December, and in a confused clash at Radcot Bridge he fled by swimming his horse across the river, dropping most of his belongings on the way, and leaving the bulk of his army to be stripped of their possessions and sent home.[28] This ignominious anticlimax was one of the crucial turning points of Richard's reign. He never forgot Radcot Bridge.

Richard was forced to accept the appeal of treason against his friends, and on 3 February 1388 opened what became known as the 'Merciless Parliament'. De Vere and de la Pole were condemned to death in their absence; Robert Tresilian, the king's chief justice, was captured during the trial, accused of giving 'aid and counsel' to the traitors, and executed;[29] Nicholas Brembre was tried and executed. The Archbishop of Canterbury protested on behalf of all clergy present that it was not permissible for them to deal with such matters.[30] But the Lords and Commons went further, impeaching more of Richard's friends and advisers, and four knights were executed in May, while two clerics were sent into exile. The knights included Sir Simon Burley, who had fought with the Black Prince at Nájera in 1367, and had been appointed Richard's tutor in his childhood; at Richard's coronation he had carried the young king on his shoulders, and in 1382 he had arranged Richard's marriage to his beloved Anne, and been rewarded with the Order of the Garter.[31] As a final act of this parliament, the Lords and Commons granted a large subsidy on wool and other goods, of which £20,000 was awarded personally to the lords who had brought the charges of treason against Richard's friends.[32]

The men who had inflicted this humiliation and loss on Richard, enriching and aggrandizing themselves in the process, were the so-called 'lords appellant' (because they had brought the appeal of treachery): Thomas, Duke of Gloucester, the king's uncle; Henry, Earl of Derby, son of John of Gaunt (Henry Bolingbroke: eventually Henry IV); Richard, Earl of Arundel (brother of Bishop Thomas Arundel); Thomas, Earl of Warwick; and Thomas, Earl Marshal. The chief architects of the whole affair were Gloucester, Arundel and Warwick; Henry Bolingbroke seems to have joined when the outcome appeared inevitable, and he pleaded unsuccessfully for the life of Simon Burley. Richard did not forget what these men had done.

However, he had learned a hard lesson, and he waited years to put it into practice.

In May 1389, when he was twenty-two, Richard belatedly declared himself of age, and announced his intention to take government of the kingdom into his own hands. He argued that the lowest man of the realm would have charge of his own affairs once in his twenties, and in this he could hardly be contradicted; he proceeded to dismiss and reappoint all the major officers of government and his household, removing the lords appellant and their followers.[33] A hostile chronicler depicted this move as petulantly immature, describing Richard's seizing the great seal and all but running out of the room with it;[34] but another suggested that 'there was none who sought to oppose the king's will . . . all praised God that He had provided them with so wise a king'.[35] It was a brilliant move on Richard's part, since it precisely challenged the basis on which power had been taken away from him in 1386 and 1388: it was not that he was essentially wilful or contemptuous of the laws of the land, but rather that he had been young and powerless. 'I have been long ruled by tutors,' he stated, neatly eliding the council for his minority with both the years of influence of his condemned favourites and the subsequent rule of the lords appellant. Now, he said, it was time for him to be a king, and there was no appetite in England to stop him.

Richard did not attempt to recall or pardon his exiled and condemned friends. In the early 1390s he reigned with apparent peace and prosperity: a truce with France was agreed and renewed, easing the pressure on taxation; John of Gaunt returned from his campaigning abroad, having been away since early 1386, and became a stabilizing influence between the king and his magnates. Richard restored Arundel, Gloucester and Henry Bolingbroke to positions of power before the end of 1389, and apparently worked in accord with his erstwhile enemies in the ensuing years. But there are one or two signs of Richard's nursing his grief, and he appears as an increasingly lonely figure. In 1390 he commissioned a book of 'miracles' said to have taken place at Edward II's tomb, with the aim of petitioning the pope for the disgraced king's canonization; he pursued the case unsuccessfully in embassies of 1395 and 1397.[36] In 1394, on the death of Queen Anne, he ordered the manor house at Sheen, where they had spent a great deal of time in recent years and where she had died, to be razed to the ground.[37] During her funeral at Westminster Abbey, one chronicler tells us, Richard thought the procession had been delayed by the Earl of Arundel, and he grabbed an attendant's cane and struck him over the head, felling him and drawing blood.[38] And in 1395 when Robert de Vere died in exile in Louvain, Richard had his body brought back to England for reburial. It is said that he had the coffin of his 'former beloved' opened, so that he could 'look upon his face, caress his fingers' before he was interred with solemn ceremony.[39]

Shortly after Anne's death, Richard departed on an expedition to Ireland, to secure the submission of the Irish lords. He took a large army, landing at Waterford in October 1394, and used it to blockade Ireland's eastern ports and to harass the countryside with raiding attacks. Before long the Irish lords of Leinster, including the self-proclaimed king of the region, had submitted to Richard and promised fealty. In January 1395 Richard wrote to Parliament to announce his success; by the spring he had received promises of obedience from all parts of his Irish lordship.[40] He had triumphed in Ireland without fighting a battle, and his sense of the majesty of kingship can only have been enhanced. These gains were temporary, however; writing a few years later, Adam Usk sharply observed that 'although the Irish pretended at the time to submit to his will, as soon as he departed news arrived that they had rebelled'.[41] Meanwhile, Richard's councillors were negotiating a new marriage for him; a Spanish match was put forward, to strengthen England's position against France. In the summer of 1395, however, the French king, Charles VI, offered his young daughter Isabella instead, as a means of contracting a long-term peace between the two countries, and the matter was agreed early in 1396.

Observers marvelled that he should have chosen to marry a seven-year-old child, meaning that at least five years would have to pass before there would be any chance of an heir.[42] In the currency of political rumour, Richard's strategy of peacemaking with England's old enemy became mixed with his difficulties at home; chroniclers writing after his fall invariably suggest that he was favourable to the French king to the extent of betraying his people, seeking his enemy's aid against his own subjects. What the marriage can be seen to signify in 1396, however, is the simple but ironic fact that Richard believed he had plenty of time. Now secure in a twenty-eight-year truce with

France, and with money flowing in from that agreement – Isabella's dowry was fixed at more than £130,000 – Richard was at the height of his power.[43] In Parliament in January 1397, he legitimized John of Gaunt's illegitimate children by his long-time companion and now wife, Katherine Swynford, stating that he did so 'with imperial power in his realm of England'.[44] There were rumours that he was being considered for election as Holy Roman Emperor, the highest status available to a European king.[45] But in the same January parliament, the Commons brought forward a bill which they put to Richard, asking among other matters 'that the great and excessive charge of the king's household should be amended and reduced'.[46] Richard replied that 'he wished to have the regality and royal liberty of his crown', and the Parliament Rolls further record his anger with the Commons:

> The king took great offence and affront in that the commons who were his lieges should wrongly take upon themselves or presume any ordinance or governance of the king's person, or his household, or other persons of standing whom it should please him to have in his company. And it seemed to the king that the commons committed a great offence therein against his regality and his royal majesty, and the liberty of himself and his honourable progenitors, which he was bound and willed to maintain and sustain by the aid of God.[47]

This was a dangerous declaration of intent, which left Parliament powerless to act. In the summer, amid a febrile atmosphere of rumour, Richard suddenly moved against his old enemies. It is said that he invited the Duke of Gloucester and Earls of Arundel and Warwick to dine with him. Gloucester pleaded ill-health, and Arundel, forewarned, simply refused; when Warwick came, Richard arrested him. He then sent Thomas Arundel, now Archbishop of Canterbury, to persuade his brother the earl to give himself up, 'promising that he would suffer no bodily harm'. He too was then imprisoned to await the next parliament. Finally, Richard took an army to Pleshey in Essex, where Gloucester was staying, and arrested his uncle. Gloucester was taken to Calais and imprisoned there.[48]

In September 1397, Richard opened what became known as the 'Revenge Parliament'. Proceedings began with an uncompromising statement of royal power: 'there would be one king and governor, and no kingdom could be governed in any other way'; 'the subjects of the kingdom should be duly obedient to the king' while 'kings should be powerful enough to govern their subjects . . . as the father teaches his son that he should abstain from vices and evils by threatening him, so the king, as a good father of all the people, should make laws by which the people may learn how to bear themselves towards him and their neighbours'. He went on to explain that the purpose of this parliament was to investigate and correct all occasions on which the prerogatives of the crown had in recent years been infringed. He promised a general pardon to follow this process, with the chilling qualification that 'fifty persons whom it would please the king to name' would not be included in that pardon, and nor would those about to be impeached.[49]

This was a hollow parody of a parliament. Richard had packed the Commons with his followers, as he had tried and failed to do with his instructions to the sheriffs in 1387. He had forbidden the Lords to bring any armed men to Westminster with them; meanwhile, he had his own army of 2,000 Cheshire archers surrounding the building. Chroniclers differ as to whether they actually began firing at one point; they were entirely at Richard's command.[50] It has been much debated whether Richard had developed a theory of royal absolutism at this time, but in any case he had certainly developed its practice. The Commons Speaker brought forward the first accusation: that in the parliament of 1386 'Thomas duke of Gloucester and Richard earl of Arundel, traitors to the king and his kingdom, by false scheming and machination caused to be made by statute a commission directed to themselves and other persons of their choosing to have the governance of the king and kingdom'. The whole of the 1386 commission was read out, in what must have been an increasingly strained and breathless atmosphere, as Richard listened once more to the words then put in his mouth about his own 'insufficient counsel and evil governance'. Finally the Speaker begged that the statute should be repealed and 'entirely annulled, as a thing made treacherously, contrary to his regality, his crown, and his dignity', which Richard was pleased to grant.[51]

This action necessarily entailed that those who had pursued and enacted the commission in 1386 were traitors for doing so. Before proceeding with that ruling, however, with scrupulous attention to procedure and existing statute, Richard repealed the royal pardons which had been granted to Gloucester, Warwick and Arundel in the Merciless Parliament of 1388, and the pardon given by charter to Arundel in April 1394, on the grounds that the king had not known 'that the matters contained in the same were so horrible and so heinous, contrary to his royal dignity'.[52]

It was in the interrogation of the three lords that Richard's depth of feeling was revealed. Arundel defended himself angrily, declaring that he was no traitor, and that Parliament itself was rigged – 'the faithful commons of the realm are not here'.[53] He accused all his detractors of lying, reserving particular venom for Henry Bolingbroke, who had turned witness against his fellow former lords appellant. Richard's judgement was implacable, rooted in his own memories, frustration and loss:

> Then the king himself said to him, 'Did you not say to me in the bath-house behind the white hall, at the time of your parliament, that there were a number of reasons why my knight Sir Simon Burley deserved to die? To which I replied that I could see no reason why he should die – but even so you and your fellows treacherously put him to death.'[54]

Arundel was beheaded, 'on the same spot hard by the Tower of London where Lord Simon de Burley had been executed'.[55] His brother the archbishop was deposed and sent into exile. On 21 September, Richard sent public word to Thomas, Earl Marshal, the Captain of Calais (the fifth lord appellant in 1388), to present the king's uncle Gloucester at Parliament for his trial; on Monday 24, the reply came and was read out:

> I am unable to cause Thomas duke of Gloucester named in the writ sent to me to come before you and your council in the present parliament, to do as the writ demands and requires, because the same duke is dead. And the same duke, by order of my most excellent lord the lord king, I had in my keeping in the prison of the lord king in the town of Calais: and he died there in the same.[56]

Gloucester had been murdered at Calais, perhaps as long as two weeks before this announcement.[57] Richard had taken the precaution of sending a man in early September to record his confession of guilt, which Gloucester was said to have written in his own hand. It was in turn read out, in English. Gloucester threw himself on the king's mercy for all offences committed, saying that he had acted 'wickedly and foolishly', but that he had meant no evil: 'truly not knowing nor witting that time that I acted against his estate nor his regality, as I did afterwards, and do now'. He added that he could not be sure what he and the others had really planned to do in 1387, ten years before, and ended with an open plea for mercy:

> But for sooth there I acknowledge, that I did untruly and unkindly as to him that is my liege lord, and hath been so good and kind lord to me. Wherefore I beseech to him notwithstanding my unkindness, I beseech him evermore of his mercy and of his grace, as lowly as any creature may beseech it unto his liege lord.

The report then reverted to French, no longer quoting Gloucester's own words. Finally, asked if he had anything to add, the duke is said to have recalled that he once 'said to the king that if he would be king, he should not seek to save the said Simon Burley from death'.[58] It is impossible not to wonder if Richard suggested or prompted this addition, drawing on another of his bitter memories. Gloucester was posthumously condemned as a traitor, all his property seized and his grants revoked. Brought in to Parliament for his own trial, the Earl of Warwick responded to these events with a full confession, and begged for mercy; Richard granted him life on the condition of perpetual imprisonment.[59]

Richard rewarded his followers lavishly at the end of September, among numerous promotions elevating the two former lords appellant who now supported him: Henry Bolingbroke became Duke of Hereford, and Thomas, Earl Marshal (who, as Captain of Calais, had seen to Gloucester's end) Duke of Norfolk.[60] Parliament was adjourned until January, when it reconvened for four days, and immediately repealed and annulled all rulings of the 1388 Merciless Parliament. Richard had his 'questions' to the judges in 1387 put again in full, and Parliament ratified that the original answers he had received had been correct in their entirety. In his great constitutional history of England, William Stubbs described this as a 'suicidal parliament', which stripped itself of its own powers, finally devolving its authority to a committee of eighteen members whom Richard believed to be his closest supporters.[61]

Over the days of his Revenge Parliament, Richard had

not only destroyed the men who had taken away his power and his friends in 1388. He had replayed events to his liking, changing history by parliamentary statute. The parliaments of 1386 and 1388 had no longer happened, in legal terms; pardons he had granted were annulled, as though they had never been. Richard therefore needed to reinforce the rulings of his present parliament in contrast, in what was an ironic foreshadowing of Henry IV's problem in 1399. How could a parliament annul parliaments without being itself vulnerable to annulment? How to be a king who has deposed a king? Richard sought to make his Revenge Parliament untouchable by obtaining the pope's confirmation of its acts, and by requiring an oath from the Lords, Commons and clergy at the tomb of St Edward, that they would uphold this parliament's statutes in perpetuity, and never revoke or annul them, on pain of excommunication. Richard turned to the Church and to the saintly king as symbolic of a higher court than any in the country, to uphold his rule.

Richard had won his revenge. But in order to do so he had needed two of the former lords appellant to break their earlier promises. He had given them pardons and promotions in recognition of their service – but he had also once pardoned the other three appellants, and now they were exiled or dead. Richard's will was sovereign, and yet it could not be trusted not to change. He had demonstrated that he would erase history, change the statutes of the realm, rather than remit his desires. By reducing Parliament to an instrument of his will, Richard sought to make all England in the image of his court, where he was sole governor – but the country could not be run like the court. The court was by definition a place of extreme instability, of faction and favourites, in which men could rise and fall as they pleased or displeased the king. For the nation to function at large, this could not be the case. The noblemen of the realm needed the security of their patrimony, their status and their rights; for them to support the king they needed to know that he would support the social structure which maintained them all. Richard had demonstrated, fatally, that everything was personal to him.

The two remaining lords appellant fell to accusing one another of treason. In Parliament in 1398, Henry Bolingbroke, Duke of Hereford, described a conversation with Thomas of Norfolk in which the latter had said 'we are about to be destroyed . . . because of what happened at Radcot Bridge'. Henry protested that they had been pardoned and forgiven, to which Norfolk insisted that 'he will do to us what he's already done to the others, because he wants to obliterate that memory'. In Henry's account of himself he continues to express pious faith in the king's goodwill, observing that Richard had sworn on St Edward to be a good lord to them; Norfolk darkly replied that he'd heard the same promises many times on the body of Christ, and he didn't trust the king any the better for them.[62]

Following this very public and serious argument, it was decreed that the two dukes should undertake a judicial combat to determine the truth of the case, as each charged the other with treason. This was a deeply uncomfortable situation for Richard, because they were effectively accusing one another of distrusting the king; whichever should triumph, the king's fidelity to his servants and theirs to him was exposed as fragile and vulnerable. Equally, he could hardly punish them without proving Norfolk right, for the crime he was accused of was that he anticipated his own and Bolingbroke's downfall at the hands of the king. Richard could not make peace with them, because they were already officially at peace and in favour with him. Repeatedly he asked them to make peace with one another – and in effect that was a plea for them to agree to declare that they trusted him, to retract the implication of their claims that the king was dangerous, rather than vying each to put the other in the king's danger – but they stood upon their honour.[63]

Richard dramatically halted proceedings moments before their combat was to take place, and – despite declaring that they were not guilty of the charges against them – pronounced sentences of banishment on the two dukes: ten years for Henry Bolingbroke, and life for Thomas of Norfolk. It is clear that there was consternation at this ruling, which insulted the honour of both men, and punished both of them for unspecified and untried crimes.[64] When Henry's father, John of Gaunt, died in February 1399, only five months later, Richard confiscated the Lancastrian lands and title, denying the exiled Bolingbroke his inheritance, to widespread condemnation. Then at the beginning of June, in a move of baffling complacency, Richard again took a large army to Ireland to try and regain the submission of the Irish lords.

Despite the size and grandeur of his army, Richard achieved little in Ireland that summer, and in Dublin in early July 1399 he received the news that Bolingbroke had landed back in England with substantial and growing forces.[65] By the time Richard had returned to Wales, around 24 July, he had already lost almost all support. Efforts to raise troops for the king proved fruitless, and his own army, brought back from Ireland, began to desert him. Panicked, he fled in the night with a few followers to Conway Castle, and the remainder of his forces disbanded entirely. Bolingbroke sent messengers to Conway, and in the absence of any alternative, Richard agreed to go to meet the duke at Flint Castle. Arriving at Flint, he saw Bolingbroke's great army gathered, and realized all was lost and that he would be taken prisoner.[66] From there he was taken to Chester, and then to the Tower of London, to await his last parliament.[67]

This became the first parliament of the reign of Henry IV. The Rolls show the somewhat laboured management of a paradox, characteristic of their difficulties as a whole: Henry's first parliament is stated to have opened on 6 October, recording that Richard had called a parliament on 30 September, which had now been rendered void by the actions of that parliament, which had deposed Richard. This meant that the parliament which had removed the king had not been called by a king, and so was not legally a parliament – but it must have been, in order to have the authority to remove him.[68] The solution was to document and ratify the 'record and process' of the deposition on the Rolls of Henry's first parliament, and to ignore the circular contradiction. Archbishop Arundel, reinstated to his see after joining with Bolingbroke on the continent, opened proceedings by declaring that

> this honourable realm of England, which is the most bountiful and well-endowed corner of the whole world . . . was on the brink of ruin, and of being most grievously and terribly destroyed and devastated, if almighty God had not through his great grace and mercy sent a wise and prudent man to govern the same realm, one who, with God's help, wishes to be ruled and advised by the wise men and elders of his realm, for his own advantage and assistance and that of all his realm.[69]

The contrast with Richard's statements of kingship could not have been clearer. A former councillor of his, William Bagot, testified that

> he had heard the king say in diverse parliaments and to diverse knights that he would have his purpose and his will of diverse matters, some in one parliament and some in another, or else he would dissolve his parliament, and when it were dissolved he would strike off their heads that were hinderers of his parliament and of his purpose.[70]

Henry promised to rule through and with Parliament, and by the advice and counsel of his magnates. In 1399, this was the only kind of kingship which could be accepted.

2
Battlefield

> He had two children by his wife, and reigned in Gascony for seven years in joy, peace and quietness . . . All men alike held him to be a great lord, faithful and wise, and I dare rightly say that since the birth of Christ there has never been such great estate kept as his, nor more honourable, for every day at table he had more than eighty knights, and four times as many squires. There were jousts and feasts in Angoulême and Bordeaux; there resided all nobility, all joy and pleasure, largesse, kindness, and honour. All his subjects and all his liegemen loved him dearly, for he did great good for them. Those who attended him prized and loved him greatly, for largesse sustained him and nobility governed him; wisdom and temperance and righteousness, reason and justice and moderation. A man could truthfully say that such a prince would not be found if the whole world were searched.
>
> The Chandos Herald on
> Edward, the Black Prince (*c.*1385)[1]

The chivalrous ideals with which Richard had been raised were ubiquitous, and formed the lifeblood of the aristocracy's claim to rule society. The literature of chivalry taught that all nobility and virtue were the property of the warrior aristocracy; in their success lay the success of the nation, and their victories brought glory. The English kings' legal claim to the throne of France provided a righteous enough cause for war, which supported the military nobility in their unending quest for fame and wealth. The cost to the French rural populace, whose lands were repeatedly ravaged and burnt, is largely incalculable; the direct cost to the English people was in contrast all too calculable, in ever-increasing taxation to fund the war. Yet the Chandos Herald, firmly rooted in the aristocratic world, could celebrate the Black Prince's extravagant rule in Gascony without ambiguity. The prince's court, like that of his father, Edward III, was modelled on the fictional glories epitomized by King Arthur, an ideal shaped in literature. The knights of the Round Table had been described and celebrated in countless French and Anglo-French romances from the twelfth century onwards, and had inspired Edward III's foundation of the chivalric Order of the Garter. Richard himself bought the *Romance of the Rose* and two romances of Gawain and Perceval in costly French manuscripts when he was thirteen.[2] Now, in the last decades of the fourteenth century, this world found its voice in English alliterative verse, in the poem now known as *Sir Gawain and the Green Knight*:

This kyng lay at Camylot upon Kryst masse
This king was at Camelot at Christmas
With mony luflych lordes, ledez of the best –
With many gracious lords, the finest people –

Rekenly of the Rounde Table alle tho rich brether –
Worthily of the Round Table, all those noble brothers-in-arms –
With rych revel oryght and rechles merthes.
With noble, fitting revelry and carefree joys.
Ther tournayed tulkes bytymez ful mony,
There warriors tourneyed on many occasions;
Justed ful jolilé thise gentyle knightes,
These noble knights jousted most joyfully,
Sythen kayred to the court, caroles to make;
Then rode to the court for ring-dances and singing.
For ther the fest watz ilyche ful fiften dayes,
For there the festivities were sustained fully fifteen days,
With alle the mete and the mirthe that men couthe avyse.
With all the feasting and the fun that men could devise.
Such glaum ande gle glorious to here,
Such noisy chatter and music, glorious to hear,
Dere dyn upon day, daunsyng on nyghtes –
A sweet din in the daytime, dancing in the nights –
Al watz hap upon heye in hallez and chambrez
All was high happiness in the halls and chambers
With lordez and ladies, as levest him thoght.
With lords and ladies, as they thought most delightful.
With all the wele of the worlde they woned ther samen,
They dwelt there together with all the good fortune in the world,
The most kyd knyghtez under Krystes Selven
The most renowned knights but for Christ Himself,
And the lovelokkest ladies that ever lif haden,
And the most lovely-looking ladies that ever lived,
And he the comlokest kyng, that the court haldes . . .
And he the most handsome king, who governs the court . . .[3]

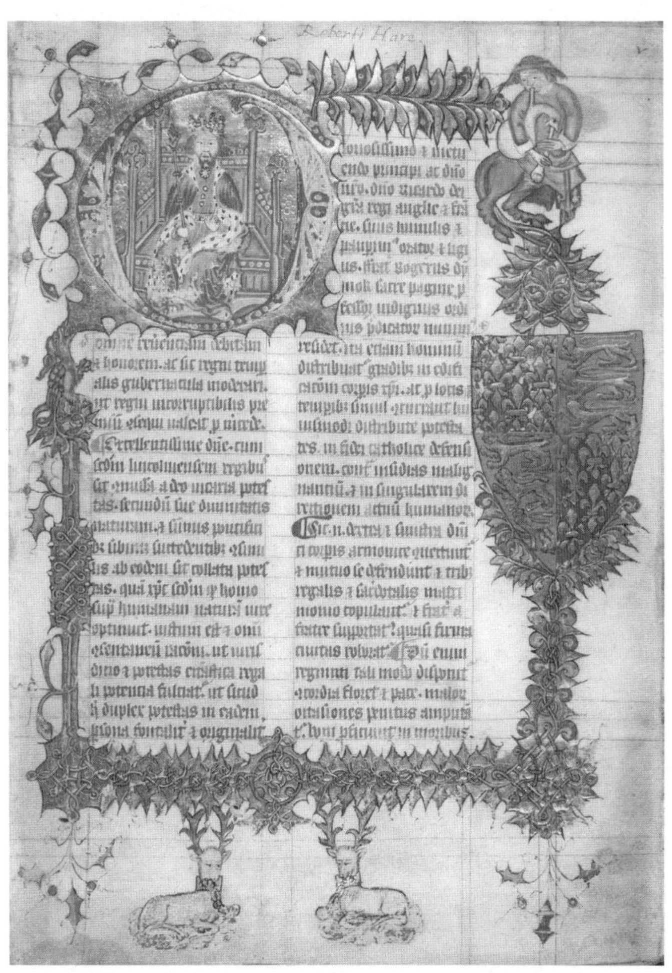

1. A gorgeously illuminated copy of the Dominican friar Roger Dymock's anti-Lollard *Treatise Against the Twelve Errors*, presented to Richard in 1394–5. Richard's symbol of the white hart appears in the lower margin, and he is shown enthroned in the decorated initial 'O', wagging an admonitory finger at heretical errors.

2. Richard kneeling, on the front left panel of the Wilton Diptych. John the Baptist indicates his blessing, alongside the Anglo-Saxon kings Edmund the Martyr (clutching the arrow symbolic of his violent death) and Edward the Confessor, whose ring suggests both the story of the saint's generosity to a beggar and Richard's own gift of a ring to Edward's shrine.

3. The white hart on the Wilton Diptych reverse, chained and collared with a golden crown – Richard's self-declared 'burden of majesty'

4. *The Way of Holding Parliament* – an idealistic work on the importance of the Commons' role in Parliament, here in a London manuscript from the time of Richard's reign

5. Westminster Hall, rebuilt at Richard's behest in the 1390s, in the form which survives today

6. A beautiful fifteenth-century imagining, from Froissart's *Chronicles*, of Richard's approach along the Thames to meet the Kentish rebels in 1381

7. Chaucer reads his tragic love story, *Troilus and Criseyde*, to the court of Richard II, as depicted in an early fifteenth-century manuscript

8. Radcot Bridge, scene of the rout of Robert de Vere and the royalist army by the lords appellant in 1387. Much of the bridge was destroyed in that clash; rebuilt six years later, it was again damaged during the Wars of the Roses, and rebuilt as it appears today.

9. The defeated Robert de Vere's flight into exile. Richard had de Vere's body returned to England upon his death in Louvain in 1395, famously opening the coffin to see his friend's face once more.

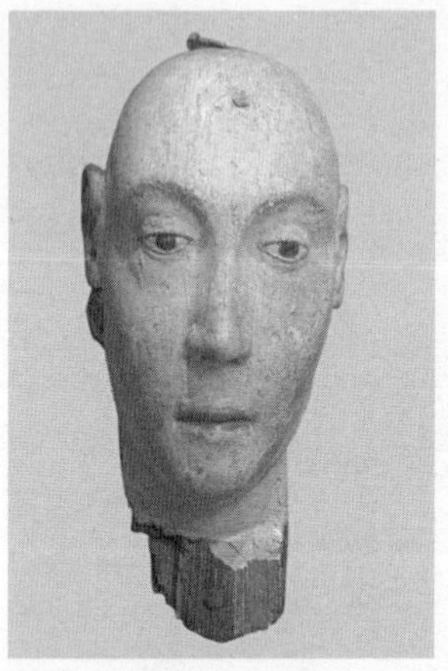

10. Head from an effigy of Anne of Bohemia, Richard's beloved first wife, probably based on her death mask

11. Richard (right) receives his child bride, Isabella of France, from her father, Charles VI.

12. The Dukes of York, Gloucester and Ireland dine with Richard II, no doubt in a rather awkward atmosphere.

13. Richard's supreme self-representation, the Westminster Abbey portrait. His apparent clean-shaven youthfulness is likely to have been an idealized invention at the time of the portrait's painting.

14. Richard is led, captive, by Henry Bolingbroke to London, to renounce the throne. Bolingbroke's armour and stature – and his army – contrast with Richard's lone, comparatively beardless figure.

15. 'With mine own hands I give away my crown': Mark Rylance as Richard II at the Globe Theatre, 2003

The Black Prince had fitted readily into this mould. A formidable military commander and charismatic leader, he had achieved the astonishing feat of capturing the King of France, forcing a treaty in 1360 by which Aquitaine became a sovereign state, wholly detached from the French crown. The profits of victory had enabled him to reward his followers handsomely, and national enthusiasm for the war was at its height while he kept his court in brilliant style. But by the time his son Richard came to the throne, the glories of Crécy (1346) and Poitiers (1356) were decades past; sovereignty over Aquitaine was effectively lost, and the war with France had lapsed into an uneasy truce, following an alarming series of English defeats and erosion of continental territory in the last years of Edward III's reign.[4] The so-called 'Good Parliament' of 1376 was a chaotic attempt at reform of royal policy, which openly acknowledged for the first time that the war was financially unsustainable. The Speaker of the Commons, Peter de la Mare,* eloquently condemned the 'diverses trespas et extorciouns' which corrupted government, saying that none of the old king's counsellors would speak truth to him, or advise him with any loyalty or wisdom, but 'every day' mocked the crown and lined their own pockets.[5] This powerful opposition focused upon the courtiers exploiting the elderly and incapable Edward III, however, and once his hated mistress Alice Perrers had been removed, and

* De la Mare was named the Commons' 'Speaker' as a matter of exigency for the 1376 parliament, but this became the office which survives today.

Richard had succeeded on the old king's death, Parliament settled somewhat. Here and throughout the reign, the tendency was to focus criticism on particular individuals charged with corruption, rather than to address the structures which made such corruption endemic.

There were plentiful reasons to object to the war in France on financial and practical grounds; more insidious was the sense that the chivalric ideal might itself be empty. With increasing force, commentators dismissed knighthood's claims to virtue as little more than a cover for greed and avarice. Battle might be glorious, but it was always bloody and terrible; victory could be a sign of God's favour, but defeat, humiliation and stalemate must therefore be the wages of sin.

> Before God all virtue is worship and all sin is shame. And in this world it is even the reverse, for the world holds them worshipful that are great warriors and fighters and that destroy and conquer many lands, and waste and give much good to those that have enough, and that spend outrageously in meat, in drink, in clothing, in building and in living in ease, sloth, and many other sins. And also the world worships them much that will be revenged proudly and pitilessly of every wrong that is said or done unto them. And of such folk men make books and songs and read and sing of them ... But whatsoever the world deemeth of such foresaid folk, learn we well that God is sovereign truth and a true judge that deemeth them right shameful before God.[6]

Churchmen had long decried the false morals of the aristocracy, but this damning description was written by a knight who had seen active service. The long story of the medieval cult of chivalry, from its emergence in the twelfth century to its belated glories in the court of the young Henry VIII, is punctuated by the ongoing conflict between knighthood's idealistic claims to virtue and divine favour, and the Church's condemnation of all chivalric values as empty and worthless. When the Black Prince had returned from France laden with gold, it was easy enough to convince the Commons of the righteousness of the English cause and the brilliance of English chivalry. With the crown near-bankrupt and the war in tatters, support for aggressive action in France was now chiefly prompted by fear that England could not defend herself against impending attack. In these circumstances, moral criticism of aristocratic dishonesty and oppression inevitably found a voice – or many voices, as happened so explosively in the revolt of 1381. Nevertheless, chivalry remained an ideal to be conjured with, an abstract value similar to kingship itself.

In the October parliament of 1377 at the beginning of Richard's reign, Peter de la Mare attacked not the order of chivalry, the high ideal which repeatedly threatened to bankrupt the country, but the corrupt conditions which, he asserted, had destroyed it. Mixing keen nostalgia for the past with condemnation of the present, he strikingly conflated the idea of 'Chivalry' with its practitioners, the group of men who claimed the title of knight:

> The noble Chivalry of the realm was long well nourished, cherished, honoured, and nobly rewarded for their great deeds, and so was knighthood most emboldened and ardently desirous of performing great enterprises and great feats of arms, each more than the other, through which the realm was greatly enriched and filled with all good things, and its inhabitants feared by their enemies . . . But now, this Chivalry has been rebuked and humiliated, and what is worse, their goods nobly won from their enemies in war have been taken from them without just cause, and furthermore knighthood and all other virtue is subject to mockery, and vice praised, advanced and honoured and in no way punished or chastised . . . so that no man today, learning from this experience, has any desire to do good: from which the Realm has now newly suffered great damage and destruction . . . and it is to be feared disaster will come if God does not make remedy of her government.[7]

It does not occur to de la Mare that there might be flaws inherent to the ideal itself. His complaint was founded in an absolute faith in chivalrous patriotism, and as a knight and Speaker of the Commons he demonstrates that this was not the sole preserve of the aristocracy. But he also displays its vulnerability, as an ideal whose practice was dependent upon good leadership and governance. This kind of moral analysis is characteristic of medieval thought: the aim is to condemn where condemnation is due, but to salvage from that criticism the ideals which animate and support society. If knighthood is failing England, then the fault must lie with particular governance, not with chivalry itself. Yet in a society so politically dependent upon the will of individuals, these notions rested permanently in paradox – what was chivalry, if not the conduct of the noblest knights? What was kingship, if not the conduct of the king? These ideological battlegrounds stood behind the open conflicts of the day, in Parliament, in the field, and on the streets of London.

In 1377 the most powerful magnates of the realm, John of Gaunt chief among them, were unwilling to abandon their military ambitions. During Richard's minority they recommitted England to the war in France, leading to a costly and inglorious sequence of advances, reverses and temporary truces, at the price of ever-heavier taxation. Dissatisfaction grew not merely at the financial cost imposed on the people, but with the sense that there was little or nothing to show for it; corruption and mismanagement were once again widely suspected. In November 1380, Parliament voted to impose a flat-rate poll tax, raised to a standard contribution of one shilling per head – three times the poll tax of 1377, and no longer (as in 1379) graded according to status.[8] This tax, and the government's increasingly punitive attempts to collect it amid unprecedented levels of evasion – one chronicler says the collectors extorted the money 'inhumanely', inflicting 'numerous injuries and intimidation'[9] – finally galvanized the rural populace into rising in rebellion. This became the Great Revolt of 1381, which turned southern England and London itself into a battlefield.

The usual term, 'Peasants' Revolt', is to some extent a misnomer, as well as an insult. The movement was driven by ambitious and educated people – businessmen, administrators, office holders, individuals of some power, wealth and influence in their local communities – and was spread from region to region by writing and preaching, in perhaps England's first demonstration of the power and danger of widespread literacy. A village only needed one person who could read in order to be a literate community, and the records of letters circulated which have survived (preserved by Latin chroniclers in the original English) have a memorable, recitable quality, deliberately echoing William Langland's great contemporary English poem *Piers Plowman*. Their tone is admonitory and apocalyptic, delivered by named leaders who are themselves symbolic of 'the people':

> Jack Carter prays you all, that you make a good end of that you have begun, and do well and ever better and better, for in the evening men reckon the day. For if the end be well, then all is well. Let Piers the Plowman my brother dwell at home and get us corn, and I will go with you and help as I may to get your meat and your drink, that ye not fail.
>
> Jack Trueman gives you to understand that falseness and guile have reigned too long, and truth has been set under a lock, and falseness reigns in every flock . . . God help us, for now is time.
>
> John Ball greets you well all and gives you to understand, he has rung our bell. Now right and might, will and skill. God speed every single one. Now is time . . . Now reigns pride on high, and covetousness is held wise, and lechery without shame, and gluttony without blame. Envy reigns

> with treason, and sloth is taken in great season. God help us, for now is time.[10]

The great rebellion began at the end of May, when a group of villagers in Brentwood, Essex, set upon one of the tax collectors, saying that they would not pay another penny (and in fact, in a claim which underlines their frustration, that they had a receipt from him to say they had already paid).[11] Uprisings swept through Essex and Kent. In early June, the king took to the Tower of London for safety, and the rebels converged on the city in their thousands. On the way they seized men they considered to be representatives of lordly oppression and publicly beheaded them; manor houses were burnt and legal documents destroyed. The revolt had taken on the character of a revolution: at a meeting on 2 June in Bocking, Essex, the rebels swore 'to destroy diverse lieges of the king and to have no law in England except only those which they themselves moved to be ordained'.[12] The fourteen-year-old king was not himself their target, for they believed him to be a natural ally of the common people; one chronicler tells us that the rebels had a 'watchword in English', 'With whom hold you?', to which the answer was 'With King Richard and with the true commons' – and anyone who did not know the correct response would be beheaded.[13]

The king offered to meet the Kentish rebels at Blackheath on 13 June, but came no further than Greenwich. They sent messengers demanding the execution of John of Gaunt and of fifteen other lords and magnates, which provided little ground for negotiation. Warned that they intended to seize him, Richard returned in alarm to the Tower, where he waited as the rebels descended upon Southwark, and broke into the Marshalsea prison (the notorious debtors' prison, to which Charles Dickens's father was sent nearly 450 years later), releasing all the prisoners. Meanwhile, another party of rebels reached Lambeth, where they raided the archbishop's palace and burned all the legal documents they could find. Finally the crowd arrived at London Bridge; the mayor hastily drew it up to keep them out, but amid some confusion (and with supporters of the rebels on both sides of the river), the drawbridge was lowered and they poured into the city. Initially little damage was done, but at Fleet Street they released all the prisoners from the Fleet Prison, and then rushed to Temple Church and destroyed the lawyers' records, setting fire to Temple Bar. Further along the Strand, they burned down John of Gaunt's manor house of the Savoy, destroying all its rich contents. One chronicler lamented the loss of what he called the finest wardrobe in Europe – hangings, ornaments, jewels and furnishings, gold and silver – but added that the rebels themselves put to death a man who tried to loot the house, declaring that they were 'zealots for truth and justice, not thieves or robbers'.[14] Their targets were specific – the legal records which they saw as tools of oppression and corruption, and the property of those whom they regarded as traitors (including the Hospital of St John, which was run by the king's treasurer, and Lambeth Palace, because the archbishop was the chancellor).

An anonymous eyewitness chronicler describes Richard

in a turret of the Tower of London, watching his city in flames around him, his counsellors lost for words.[15] By this account, the distraught king proclaimed a universal amnesty, if the rebels would only go home peacefully and put their grievances in writing to him – an offer which they dismissed as 'trifles and mockery'. The well-informed French chronicler Jean Froissart (1337?–*c.*1404) contrastingly describes a detailed debate in the Tower between Richard's advisers, on the possibility of resisting the rebels by force – in the Tower garrison, and at various noblemen's lodgings, there were hundreds of men-at-arms and knights available to command.[16] But they could not know which side the mass of Londoners would take, and in any event, the outcome would be bloody and destructive. Men on horseback are at a sudden disadvantage in the narrow streets of a city; a mob on foot can move much faster and to greater effect. After lengthy deliberation they sent messages that the king would meet with the commons at Mile End, which (by no coincidence) was some distance out of the city. At that meeting, on 14 June, the king diplomatically conceded all the rebels' demands as a matter of the process of law, the execution of traitors being their foremost concern – but if Richard hoped his promises of future trials would quell the present violence, he was mistaken. Either as he negotiated at Mile End, or shortly afterwards, a group of rebels broke into the Tower and ran riot through it, eventually seizing and beheading the king's chancellor, Simon Sudbury, Archbishop of Canterbury, and Sir Robert Hales, the king's treasurer.

Richard called the rebels to another meeting at

Smithfield the following day. Overnight many more buildings were burnt and people killed, including a direct attack on the foreign residents of London, craftsmen who competed for business with the Londoners. In 1377 Flemish and Brabant clothmakers in London had officially been taken under the king's protection.[17] Nevertheless, thirty-five Flemings seeking sanctuary that night were notoriously dragged out of the Church of St Martin Vintry (later destroyed in the Great Fire of 1666), and killed. Rebels from the counties can have had no motivation for this; evidently some Londoners took advantage of the chaos to pursue their own violent ends.

At Smithfield on 15 June, Richard faced a great host of rebels and their leader, Wat Tyler, who came forth to speak to him. All the chroniclers recount with distaste Tyler's arrogant lack of regard for the king's majesty – he carried a dagger, demanded and drank a cup of ale, and supposedly sought to start a fight with one of the king's men. This was an excuse to call for his arrest, and in the ensuing scuffle Tyler was killed. Now came King Richard's moment: his one extreme act of bravery, on an effective battlefield, which averted disaster. As the rebels realized their leader was dead, and began to raise their bows and staves and prepare to fight, Richard rode out to them and into the host, shouting that he was their king, and they could not wish to harm him; meanwhile his party sent word that Richard was in peril and in need of support from all London. Richard ordered the rebels out to meet him again in the field of St John in Clerkenwell (now just around the corner from Farringdon tube station);

once again, the aim was to remove them from the city. There, struck by uncertainty in the absence of their leader, intimidated by the arrival of many of the mayor's men, and mollified by Richard's repeated promises of justice and amnesty, they began to disperse.

This may have been the defining event of Richard's life. The fourteen-year-old king showed undoubted courage and determination, and he won a great victory, riding among a crowd of his people. But if this day was formative, it was not unambiguously positive. No king should seek a victory over his own people, or have brought about a situation where one was necessary. Richard may never have understood this. In a letter of 1398 refusing to send military aid or money to an ally abroad, he explained:

> some of our subject magnates and nobles ... have made many attempts on the prerogative and royal right of our regal state, and have wickedly directed their malevolence even against our person. Wherefore when we could no longer endure their rebellion and wantonness, we collected the might of our prowess, and stretched forth our arm against these our enemies; and at length, by the aid of God's grace, we have by our own valour trodden on the necks of the proud and the haughty, and with a strong hand have ground them down, not to the bark only, but even to the root; and have restored to our subjects peace.[18]

Richard's 'peace' was submission to his will, and to the majesty of kingship. His success at Smithfield was undoubtedly shaped by the careful planning of his counsellors, but it also allowed the youthful Richard to believe that he alone had saved the kingdom. If the anonymous eyewitness and Froissart's accounts of the days in the Tower are combined, we have a picture of an isolated and stricken young king, ill-advised or contrarily advised (or ignored?) by his counsellors, who eventually rode out alone to speak to his people and convince them of his good faith. But if this was how Richard remembered it, he chose not to remember a great deal. The king's party may well have planned Tyler's death; the other rebel ringleaders were later rounded up and executed, and all concessions Richard made to the commons were repealed in Parliament the following month.[19] Richard himself took part in a 'visitation' of Essex to crush the remnants of rebellion there, and apparently dismissed their spokesmen with threats of death, as 'wretches . . . unworthy to live': 'you will be forever in bondage, not as you have been, but incomparably more vilely'.[20] A scrap of an English poem survives in a Cambridge University manuscript from the early fifteenth century:

Man be war and be no fool:
Thenke apon the ax, and of the
  stool. *executioner's block*
The stool was hard, the ax was
  scharp
The iiii yere of kyng Richard.[21] *fourth*

Froissart said that more than fifteen hundred people across the country were beheaded, hanged or otherwise put to death.[22]

The rebels had sought to seal a bond of trust between the commons and the king, against lordly oppression. Richard had had no such bond in mind. For Richard, his triumph proved the untouchable nature of kingship. Contrarily, the government's reassertion of control over England in the aftermath demonstrated a merciless insistence on the social structure, which tied all into the hierarchy, supporting the king at the top. It was a part of Richard's failure that he did not understand, or would not accept, his throne's dependence on the stability of that structure.

In 1385, when he was eighteen, Richard undertook the military expedition intended to be his chivalric coming of age. For the first time in half a century, the army was assembled by a general feudal levy: lords were enjoined upon their 'fealty and homage' to come to the king's summons with their men. This was an archaic formulation, and one not upheld by the eventual form of the army, which was composed largely of men serving as professional paid soldiers. Nevertheless, at the end of July an army of perhaps 14,000 men was mustered at Newcastle-upon-Tyne, ready to march into Scotland, where a small force of French men-at-arms had joined the Scots in launching incursions into northern England – as a distraction from simultaneous French planning for an invasion of the south coast. The latter threat was infinitely greater, and indeed Richard had been promised funding for his expedition the previous year on the understanding that he would launch a continental invasion. In this context the use of the feudal levy seems to have been solely a ploy to raise money from scutage (the monetary payment due in lieu of feudal service), since Parliament would revoke the funding it had offered rather than spend it on a Scottish war.[23] In the event scutage was not collected, no doubt because it would have sparked a crisis of resistance, and the Scottish expedition was an anticlimactic raid.

Deprived of full-scale battle by the entirely predictable tactical retreat of the Scots and their French allies, and running desperately short of provisions in a countryside already stripped to hinder their advance, the English resorted to burning and ravaging what they could find, destroying the Abbeys of Dryburgh, Melrose and Newbattle on the thin pretext that their inhabitants supported the French antipope Clement VII. Reaching Edinburgh, Richard still found no Scottish army to fight. Several chroniclers suggest that John of Gaunt then advised marching further into Scotland, to take the entire country by force, but that Richard angrily accused him of disloyalty for suggesting such a dangerous strategy, in the absence of reliable provisions.[24] Meanwhile, the French and Scots had cut round to the west and sacked Carlisle, nearly a hundred miles away.[25] In any case, Richard turned home, with little to show for his adventures, but also without major losses or humiliation. In great part this was accidentally owed to the people of Ghent, whose temporary seizure of the Flemish port of Damme threatened the French hold on the coast, and necessarily distracted the French king from his plans for an invasion of England until too late in the year for a fleet to sail.

Richard's expedition of 1385 had carried all the trappings of noble chivalry; he had created numerous knights, dukes and earls in the field, and expected these awards to be ratified by Parliament in the autumn. But the Commons were critical of Richard's extravagance, not least because his grandfather had always brought such promotions to Parliament first. In his charters, Richard explained his flurry of pre-emptive patronage with formulaic rhetoric:

> A country resplendent with noblemen who excel not only in mature counsel but in vigour of arms is certain to be happy. For just as the sky is rendered bright and clear by the stars, so not only kingdoms but kingly diadems reflect the light of dignity . . .[26]

Such numerous elevations entailed promises of thousands of pounds' being paid direct from the Treasury, in order to sustain the new dukes and earls in the manner expected of their status. It was not merely the cost to royal finances which rankled with the Commons, however; Richard promoted men far beyond their inherited station, in a challenge to that same social hierarchy which guaranteed his own status. Towards the end of the 1385 parliament, he gave his favourite, Robert de Vere, Earl of Oxford, the new rank of 'Marquess of Dublin', using a title unprecedented in England, and presented him with the lordship of Ireland.[27] This extreme honour made him superior to all other earls, and had evidently arisen from no particular virtue the man possessed, but solely from the king's affection for a friend from boyhood. Despite Parliament's disapproval, Richard went on to make de Vere 'Duke of Ireland' the following year, in a dramatic demonstration of his disregard for the Commons' criticisms, which led directly to the 'Wonderful' and 'Merciless' parliaments that followed.[28]

In times of truce – for peace was a rare thing in this period – the military aristocracy sought ritualized training for the battlefield as well as leisure in the tournament. The celebratory moments of Richard's reign show his deployment of chivalric display to his own aggrandizement. In 1386 and 1390, he held great tournaments at Smithfield; on the latter occasion, the festivities lasted several days and were attended by many foreign dignitaries, chiefly French nobility. The codes of chivalry found no irony in the warm welcome and sporting contests offered to the country's aristocratic enemies, though the fifteenth-century English chronicler of the event may have shown his sensitivities by referring to all the visitors simply as 'strangers', foreigners.[29] Richard did not take part in tournaments himself, as his father and grandfather had done;[30] his role was gloriously to preside.

> These jousts and tournament were held at London in Smithfield, for all manner of foreigners . . . and to them and to all others the household was held open with great feasts, and also great gifts were given . . . And those of the king's side were all of one suit: their coats, their armour, shields, and their horses and trappings were all adorned with white harts, with crowns around their necks, and chains of gold hanging thereupon, and the crown hanging low before the

> hart's body. This hart was the king's livery that he gave to lords and ladies, knights and squires, in order to know his household from others. And at this first coming to the jousts, twenty-four ladies led the twenty-four Lords of the Garter with chains of gold, and all in the same suit of harts as aforementioned, from the Tower on horseback through the city of London into Smithfield, where the jousts were held.[31]

The ride from the Tower to Smithfield must have brought to Richard's mind the tumultuous events of nine years earlier. Now all was peaceful, with cheering crowds, the flower of English chivalry decked in Richard's newly adopted symbol of the white hart,[32] and the nobles of France admiring the majesty of England.

The white hart appears as Richard must have commissioned it on the reverse of the Wilton Diptych, seated on a bed of rosemary, collared with a crown with a long gold chain. It was the noblest beast of the hunt, and a figure for Christ in its suffering. Richard's hart (the pun was no doubt intended and often used) apparently bears majesty as a noble burden, the deer's white coat a sign of purity, the rosemary for remembrance of sorrow: and indeed in his will, drafted in 1399, Richard observed 'how, since our tender age . . . [we have] submitted our neck to the burden of royal rule'.[33] On the opposite panel were Richard's royal arms impaled with the arms of St Edward the Confessor (a later confection, since heraldry postdated the Anglo-Saxon king). Between the two symbols, the arms impaled with the saint's and the grieving hart, Richard could hardly have been clearer about his idiosyncratic understanding of heraldic display. There was no reference to martial prowess here. Richard's use of symbolism was a part of the aura of pious kingship, illuminating its inherent holiness and nobility; it directed the audience towards the higher significance of the king's historical inheritance, and the touch of the divine.

Yet Richard used his livery as cynically as any other lord. In the latter years of his reign he worked hard to build up an 'affinity' – a group of sworn knights and men-at-arms from all parts of the country, carrying his livery badge, who would support him in times of danger as an effective small standing army, a praetorian guard.[34] In this he copied the conduct of his magnates, and the Commons in Parliament repeatedly tried to limit the use of such livery badges, complaining of the 'great and outrageous oppressions' committed in the countryside by lawless armed men, 'the more emboldened and encouraged in their maintenance and evil deeds because they are of the retinue of lords'.[35] Richard offered to ban the use of livery badges, but it may have been an empty gesture, and in any case the Lords resisted it. In the event, the measures taken to restrict the use of livery to higher status retainers, with whom the lord had genuine and lasting bonds, benefited Richard above all, and he retained and expanded his own affinity throughout the 1390s. His particular love of Cheshiremen over all other regions brought consternation among the people; his private army of Cheshire archers (and apparently axemen) consistently numbered several hundred, all of whom followed him around the country in the years after 1397, when he had brought as many as 2,000 of them to Parliament.[36] An anonymous English poet writing after Richard's fall sorrowfully explained how his proud retinue of armed men had alienated the rest of his people:

They plucked the plumage from the poor's skins,
And showed their signs for men should dread — *livery badges*
To ask any mends for their misdeeds.
Thus liveries overlooked your lieges each one; — *scorned*; *subjects*
For those that had harts on high on their breasts,
For the more partie, I may well avow, — *For the most part*
They bore them the bolder for their gay brooches,
And bushed with their breasts and bore down the poor — *thrust out their chests*
Lieges that loved you the less for their evil deeds.
So, truth to tell, as town-men said,
For one that ye marked, ye missed ten score
Of homely hearts that the harm hente . . . — *simple*; *suffered*
I not what you ailed, but if it ease were; — *I don't know what was wrong with you*

For first at your anointing all
were your own,
Both harts and hinds, and held of
none other;
No lede of your land but as a liege ought, *person / as a subject should [be]*
Till ye, of your dullness,
disseverance made.[37]

The people were familiar with and accepting of lordly retinues, much as they disapproved of their violent behaviour. But for the king to make some men his own, to give some few people his badge to wear, was to distance himself intolerably from the rest of his subjects – in the poet's words, for each man he favoured he missed two hundred others who might have loved him. Richard appeared as a man who expected to fight his own people, even while he sought conciliation and peace with foreign enemies.

Richard was not alone in desiring peace with France, but his reasons for doing so may have been idiosyncratic. In 1395 he received an open 'letter' from the French soldier and diplomat Philippe de Mézières, a lengthy plea to the Kings of England and France to abandon their war and turn, as allies, to the matter of Holy War in the East. The crusading ideal remained strong in the later fourteenth century, but Richard himself never seems to have been tempted. Philippe may have hit nearer the mark with a startling moment in his letter, when he argued that 'if the two kings make war on each other, they will become the serfs of all their subjects'. It is 'impossible to satisfy the will of men-at-arms'; a prince who achieves victory in war risks the sins of 'vainglory, outrageous pride, presumption and avarice', while one who allows his generals to go into battle on his behalf is thrown into servitude if they succeed, in an enterprise which is in any case sinful:

> Oh, what evil royal servitude before God! The more Christian souls the aforesaid commander has sent into hell, the more the king becomes his serf. And if the king does not reward the commander as he wishes, he becomes indignant, and perhaps secretly forms a group of his own – the effect of which in the future, to the prejudice of the royal majesty, need not be spoken of further.[38]

This is little more than an encouragement to kingly paranoia. It must have appeared a clever and uncontroversial argument to Philippe: Christians should not slaughter one another, pride is a sin, chivalric competition over worldly glories can lead to conflict – all of which supported his call for a crusading expedition. But perhaps all Richard saw, in the beautifully illustrated presentation copy he was sent,[39] was the constant threat to his dignity posed by the military and political ambitions of his magnates and lords. Chivalry had long been the most expensive business in the world; kings had bankrupted themselves at war, and landless princes had bankrupted themselves supporting their followers, hosting feasts and tournaments. It took a particular genius and a great deal of luck to make war pay, and Richard had neither.

Richard understood the glorious display of chivalry, and the necessity of largesse, by which the prince rewarded his most worthy followers, and his and their glittering successes reflected light to shine the brighter upon one another. What he lacked was the substance of military victory, and the discernment of whom to reward. When he took his fateful expedition to Ireland in 1399, he was perhaps seeking to rekindle the sense of victory he had gained from the submission of the Irish nearly five years before. He had not fought a battle then, and he did not fight one now. By the time he returned to England, the country was already lost. As in 1399, so in the conflict at Radcot Bridge in 1387: when the critical moments of his reign turned on a battlefield, Richard wasn't there.

3
City

Memorandum that on the Friday after the Feast of Epiphany [6 January] this year [1382] the Mayor, aldermen and the commons were arrayed to ride in procession with the queen, the Emperor's sister, and whereas all the city misteries were instructed that their clothing must be of red and white, the goldsmiths were dressed in these same colours, and since all the other misteries had various cognizances, the goldsmiths had the red part of their clothing barred with silver wire and powdered with silver pearl trefoils, and each of the seven score men of the said mistery wore on their left side a large gold clasp with gemstones, and on their heads they wore chaplets covered in red material powdered with the said trefoils, and they rode with the queen throughout the city, and the said wardens paid various expenses for the said riding as follows:

Firstly, to the 6 minstrels – 60s
Item, for the clothing of the same minstrels – 24s 5d
Item, for leaves to be diapered[1] to throw over the queen – 5s
Item, for silvered skins – 3s 4d
Item, to the porter of St Bartholomew's and his servant – 14d

Item, to a painter for the minstrels' ornaments – 2s 2d
Total: £4 16s 1d

Memorandum also that a summer-castle was set up in Cheap and well decorated, and three virgins leaned out of it to throw leaves, and this castle cost:

Firstly, for 6 yards of red cloth at 18d the yard –
1¼ yards of red cloth at 30d the yard –
3 yards of white cloth at 28d the yard –
John Garoun, for carpentry work – 43d.[2]

The guilds or 'misteries' of London (so-called because of the secrets of their crafts, which were revealed only to apprentices) kept detailed records of their business. At the age of fifteen in 1382, Richard brought his sixteen-year-old bride, Anne of Bohemia, with ceremonial procession into London, culminating in their marriage and her coronation. The goldsmiths had a central part to play in organizing the festivities. The English *Brut* chronicler notes that 'the people of the city . . . Mayor and aldermen and all the commons, rode to her to welcome her, and every man in good array, and every craft with its minstrelsy, in the best manner'.[3] The goldsmiths' account books supply detail to this, in pounds, shillings and pence, and reading them now gives something of a frisson: this is private information about the hidden workings of the show they put on, revealing a whole new layer of life in the city. Looking at the first set of charges, we can see that musical and artistic talent was highly prized – and the minstrels were not expected to fund their own ceremonial clothing, worth more than half their pay. Perhaps the porter of St Bartholomew's gave his servant a few pence from his share, while the skilled carpenter John Garoun earned three times as much for his work, which must surely have taken a few days. Someone with a keen eye had noted that the bulk of the wooden model castle could be draped with the cheaper red cloth, as long as a few feet of the expensive stuff took centre stage. Perhaps the three maidens in the tower were so honoured to be part of the celebration, chosen ahead of their peers, that they required no pay; fortunate, because collecting and decorating the leaves they threw, confetti-style, cost a whole five shillings.

This was a period of astonishing disparities in wealth and living. A typical workman's daily wage in the 1380s was 4d, giving an annual income of around £5 (100s), assuming he could find work at least 300 days a year; a gallon of good ale cost just over a penny, as did two chickens or two dozen eggs. In London a goose was supposed to cost 6d, but sharp-eyed salesmen often asked seven or eight. A year's tuition at Oxford University in 1374 cost 26s 8d, though lodgings there were significantly pricier at 104s a year (when annual rent for a cottage might be 5s, or 20s for a craftsman's house), and the student would need 40s for his clothing. Meanwhile a merchant's house in London (such as the one in which Geoffrey Chaucer was born) might be rented for two or three pounds a year, which was about what it would cost to send your son to a monastery school. Higher up the social scale, the numbers lose purchase. A knight's two horses, without which he couldn't function as a knight, would cost him about £10.

His armour could total nearer £20. In 1397 Thomas, Duke of Gloucester owned armour worth £103. If a man were attendant at court he would need a fashionable gown, in silk or fur: it would certainly cost £10, and he could easily spend £50. The life annuity granted to Chaucer in 1367 (paid until 1388), of £13 6s 8d, would make him wealthy in the city of London, yet would barely support him at all at court. But as a courtier he was the recipient of largesse – robes, livery, gifts – and appointments to administrative offices from which, it was understood, he would profit. In 1389 Richard II made Chaucer Clerk of the King's Works in London; in 1393 he presented him with £10 as a gift for good service, and in 1394 awarded him an annuity of £20.[4]

Chaucer becomes an interesting figure from this perspective, standing between the court and the city, moving upward with his talents and the notice of powerful men, but always vulnerable to the changing favours and factions of politics.[5] One early fifteenth-century manuscript of his masterpiece *Troilus and Criseyde* has a gorgeous frontispiece which depicts him reading to a group of lords and ladies in a garden, outside a beautiful castle, with a procession in the background.[6] He stands in a raised wooden pulpit decorated with scarlet cloth, but he himself is drably clothed in comparison with the luminous figures surrounding him. The Chaucer who became celebrated as the 'father of English literature' was a product of his later fifteenth-century poetic followers; the fourteenth-century man who served the king on diplomatic missions abroad and in administrative roles in London and Kent, while writing with unmatched genius in new forms of English verse, is much harder to grasp. Notoriously his writings provide little or no access to his personal life; his gaze was turned outward, to the world around him, and beyond that to the realm of imagination, seeing inside the minds of others. Chaucer's city is glimpsed in the Canterbury pilgrims' gathering at the Tabard Inn in Southwark, and the ebullient Host, Harry Bailly, who sets them their storytelling challenge. The short stub of 'The Cook's Tale', cut off after fewer than sixty lines, depicts a young apprentice keener on the festivities – and women – of London than on his work:

> He was as full of love and paramour
> As is the hive full of honey sweet;
> Well was the wench with him might meet.
> At every bridal would he sing and hop; *wedding party*
> He loved better the tavern than the shop.
> For when there any riding was in Cheap, *Cheapside*
> Out of the shop thither would he leap –
> Till that he had all the sight y-seen
> And dancèd well, he would not come again –
> And gathered him a mesnée of his sort *company*
> To hop and sing and maken such disport.[7]

When the apprentice's master grows exasperated with his behaviour and throws him out, he moves in with a friend whose wife keeps a shop for the look of the thing, but actually works as a prostitute – and there the little story ends abruptly, unfinished. This is another London, seen from beneath, but nevertheless participating in the spectacle and festival of the grand pageants, tournaments and ceremonies; these are the people who cheered in the streets as Richard and his bride rode past.

Shakespeare's Prince Hal memorably moves through the London of taverns and whorehouses, but Richard II in literature and in life can barely be imagined in such a setting. He did, however, try to involve himself in London politics, often punishing the city for episodes of disorder, and he expected the Londoners' support at times of difficulty, with unreliable results.[8] He repeatedly intervened in mayoral elections, which were riven by faction throughout the period; in 1384 he supported the mayor, Nicholas Brembre, in a showpiece summary trial and execution of one of his rival's supporters:

> Richard, by the grace of God etc. . . . when of late a great outbreak of our people, against our peace, was threatened in our city . . . one John Constantyn, cordwainer, [is charged with] going among, counselling, comforting, and inciting the people of the said city to close their shops, and through his iniquitous contrivances, in the way of rumour, commotion, disturbance, and insurrection . . . he was therefore taken . . . and upon this was recently arraigned, and on the testimony of witnesses sworn and examined, and upon his own acknowledgement thereon, and for other reasons, sentenced to death, and beheaded; – we would ratify and confirm the judgement given in this behalf . . . by way of strengthening from henceforth the governance of the said city . . .[9]

No doubt he expected complete loyalty from the men he supported in this way, and Nicholas Brembre obliged, only to pay for it with his life in the Merciless Parliament of 1388.[10] Richard appeared not to understand the costs of his involvement in vicious factional politics. It was as an intimate of Richard's hated inner circle that Brembre lost his post as mayor in 1386, and was arrested for treason the following year. In that crisis of 1387 as he prepared to face the lords appellant in a hostile parliament, Richard sent for the new mayor, Nicholas Exton, and his aldermen to ask how many men-at-arms they could muster to come to his aid. They replied 'that the inhabitants of the city were in the main craftsmen and merchants, with no great military experience, and it was not permissible for them to devote themselves to warfare save for the defence of the city alone'.[11] The substantive message here was that the Londoners would not fight for Richard in a civil struggle against his own magnates, a rebuff which no doubt contributed to his later concerted attempts to build up an affinity of retainers. Richard expected love and loyalty from the Londoners, and apparently could not see the necessary limits of that bond. More critically for a king who sought the affection of his people, Richard's actions acknowledged no difference between outward action and inward feeling. At the same time he issued a proclamation in London in English:

> Our Lord the King, that God save and watch over, commandeth to all his true lieges in the city of London, and the suburb, of what condition that ever they be, upon the pain

> of their lives, and forfeiture of their goods, that none be so hardy to speak, nor act, nor publish, in private nor openly, anything that might imply evil or dishonesty of our liege Lord the King, nor of our Lady the Queen, or any lords that have been dwelling with the King by for this time . . . nor that none of his true lieges trouble themselves with such matters, but that our Lord the King, our sovereign judge, must ordain thereof that to him seemeth best.[12]

This order simply demanded a show of loyalty and obedience, rather than trying to win or to earn such devotion. It instructed the Londoners that it was not for them to consider or to judge the conduct of their betters – but this was an order at odds with the city's power and importance as the engine of the realm, and it was cited in Brembre's trial as evidence of his tyrannous misconduct.[13] The ruling men of London were powerfully aware of the city's status, which emerges in their records and ordinances as the condition under which all judgements are made:

> There is a greater resort, as well of lords and nobles, as of common people, to that city, than to any other places in the realm . . . and therefore there is the greater need of good governance therein, and of peace, in especial; and more particularly . . . it is the capital city and the watch-tower of the whole realm, and . . . from the government thereof other cities and places do take example . . . [14]

The support of the city was vital to political success at various moments of crisis. William Langland called the

Mayor of London the *meene*, the mediator between king and commons.[15] Richard thought of London as 'his' city; beyond his reach, however, it was powerfully its own city, and the independence and entitlement of the Londoners did not go unnoticed elsewhere in England. When Brembre was executed in 1388, a Leicester chronicler recorded some wild rumours which neatly encapsulate his critical view of Richard and of his supporters in London:

> Brembre had perpetrated many oppressions and seditions in the city. It was said of him that when he was at the height of his power as mayor he set up a public block and axe to chop off the heads of those who rose against him . . . And it was said that he proceeded against 8,500 or more of his opponents . . . [and] he would have had them all beheaded . . . If he had lived he would have had himself made duke of Troy by the king, for in ancient times London was called the second Troy, and so he would have been the duke of London, the name of London being changed to Troy.[16]

Here Brembre is accused of terror and tyranny, and the king associated with these horrors by implication. The identification of London with Troy had originated with Geoffrey of Monmouth's twelfth-century Latin *History of the Kings of Britain*, a fantastical pseudo-history tracing the origins of Britain's kings back to the Trojan prince Brutus; a poet writing in the 1390s for Richard II could still call London 'New Troy'.[17] Geoffrey's work, rapidly translated into French and English and soon spawning a whole romance literature, had popularized the glory of King

Arthur, whom medieval English kings had long claimed as an antecessor. Richard's own inspirations were more pious and pacific figures, but the notion that Richard might have renamed London 'Troy' and presented it as a dukedom to his favourite is not an entirely ridiculous accusation in wider context. Richard was the king who arbitrarily appointed his friend Robert de Vere 'Duke of Ireland' in 1386, and in 1397 made Chester a principality, setting it above all other regions, with a machinery of government modelled on that of England itself, because he bore such affection for the city and its men. This astonishing, even bizarre favouritism to some places and people, at the literal and symbolic expense of others, would bring about his downfall.[18]

In 1392 Richard came head to head with the mayor and aldermen of London, enraged at the city's refusal to lend him a large sum of money (variously described by the chroniclers as between £1,000 and £5,000). The specific details of the case cannot be ascertained, but certainly Richard was in financial need throughout these years, and both the city and individual Londoners had become much less willing to lend since the upheavals of 1386–8.[19] A chronicler based in the monastery at St Albans, Thomas Walsingham (*c.*1340–*c.*1422), took the opportunity of recounting Richard's dispute with the city to express an apparently long-nurtured resentment against Londoners, calling them 'the haughtiest, the most arrogant, and the most avaricious of all the peoples of the world', who had passed civic laws by which 'they harassed, oppressed and vexed visitors from surrounding towns and districts. I pass over their inhumanity, I say nothing of their greediness, I make no mention of their untrustworthiness, I remain silent about their malice, which they practised indiscriminately against people who came to London.'[20] The reader is compelled to speculate on the nature of Thomas's own visits to the city which so enraged him.

A more sympathetic – and Westminster-based – chronicler, writing of the events of 1392, agreed that the Londoners had refused to make Richard a large loan, and explained that the king had turned instead to an Italian banker, who quickly obliged. When the king asked him how he had sourced the funds, however, the Italian said he'd borrowed it from various London merchants, and Richard felt humiliated.[21] Whatever the immediate cause of Richard's indignation – and there was another outbreak of violence in London's streets that spring – he suddenly declared in May 1392 that his courts, Exchequer, chancery and several other government offices should all be moved from Westminster to York.[22] This was a shocking thing to do; the machinery of government had been located in York as a matter of strategy during the height of Edward I's and Edward III's Scottish wars, but all these offices had resided in Westminster for more than half a century at this point.

Meanwhile, Richard summoned London's leaders to attend him in Nottingham in June, where he accused them of misgovernance and removed the mayor and two sheriffs from office. In July he revoked all of London's ancient liberties and privileges by royal decree. Then at Windsor on the 22nd, the Londoners appeared before the king to receive his judgement, making humble entreaties for pardon. Thomas Walsingham, contemptuous as ever, tells us that he sent them away with the full weight of their punishment, including a vast fine, and adds (ridiculously) that the king considered raising an army to launch an assault upon the city and 'annihilate' its citizens. At length, however, hearing of the sorrow and suffering of the people, Richard magnanimously declared: 'I will go to London, and console the citizens, and will not allow them to despair any more of receiving my pardon.'[23] The more balanced Westminster chronicler describes the queen's prostrating herself before the king to beg for mercy on behalf of the city.[24] This may well have occurred, and if so it would certainly have been staged with Richard's foreknowledge; the lady's duty of persuading her lord to be merciful was a cliché of the Middle Ages.[25] Gestures are repeated in literature because they possess power in reality; life may well have echoed art here, and Richard was a lover of ritualized display.

In any case, Richard's 'mild and kindly nature was moved by pity', and he 'forgave the Londoners all their offences against him on condition that within the next ten years they paid him . . . £40,000'.[26] We might not all hope for such forgiveness, but Richard cannot have anticipated collecting the whole sum. His immediate focus – impractical though it seems – was on his other demand, for a royal progress into the city with all ceremony and festivity, which took place on 21 August 1392, ten years after his royal entrance with Anne, and fifteen years after his coronation procession. Once again the streets were decorated and decked in fine cloths; the king and queen were showered with gifts;

temporary structures put up in the streets carried little boy angels, who crowned Richard and Anne with gold, all the while singing. The procession ended at the shrine of Edward the Confessor in Westminster Abbey, where Richard greeted his saintly predecessor. The following day the Warden of London invited Richard to a vast banquet, where he was presented with further gifts.[27] Richard restored London's liberties in September – on the promise of good behaviour – and court and chancery were all back in Westminster by Christmas. Nevertheless, he insisted on the vast sum of £10,000 as the cost of his forgiveness, and appears to have received it in February 1393.[28] The Londoners' faithful love and their money were both important to Richard; unfortunately he sought the latter at the expense of the former, while imagining them to be the same thing.

In 1398 Richard wrote to ask the details of the arrest in London of a carter named John Sewale, and why he had been detained in Newgate Prison. The mayor's reply put the matter very simply, in careful legal terms, stating that he had been accused before mayor, recorder, sheriffs and coroner by a certain Richard Hawtyn of Gloucester, who

> appealed John Sewale, *cartere*, of Iseldone [Islington], because that he, the aforesaid John Sewale, on the 15th day of the month of September, in the 21st year of the reign of King Richard the Second, in the Church of St Martin le Grand, in London, did say to Richard Hawtyn aforesaid, that there had been no peace or love in England since the present King of England became king; and in like manner, did further say that he is not the rightful king.[29]

These are not words a king would wish to see in writing, and it was not the first time someone had been arrested for seditious speech. In 1391 a man named William Mildenhall had appeared in chancery accused of having concealed the fact that his father 'had spoken disrespectfully' of the king, saying that he was 'unfit to govern and should stay in his latrine'.[30] On that earlier occasion Richard mercifully released Mildenhall. Sewale was not so lucky, being arraigned and condemned to prison before the chief men of the city. Richard's grip on London was tightening; in 1397 he bypassed the usual election procedures and simply appointed his own favourite as mayor, Richard Whittington (no cat appears in the chronicles). It was Whittingon who negotiated a 'solution' to the five-year-old question of London's liberties, having them restored in perpetuity (rather than 'until the king should ordain otherwise') in return for yet another 'loan' of 10,000 marks (£6,666 13s 4d), which was never paid back.[31] Yet despite Richard's constant and punitive demands on the city, it often demonstrated its loyalty to him. In 1399 the Londoners did not make peace with Bolingbroke until Richard was his prisoner. Notably, the Lancastrian lord landed in the north on his return from exile and did not attempt to approach London,[32] instead waiting for the aldermen of the city to come to him.

Despite his apparent switch of favour to York to punish London in 1392, Richard's relationship with the former was much weaker, and the feeling was mutual. The Great Revolt was largely a southern phenomenon,[33] but the inhabitants of York resisted the poll tax in other ways – the population of 7,248 in 1377 had apparently mysteriously fallen to 4,015 in 1381. Yorkshire as a whole declared only 55 per cent of the 1377 population in the 1381 tax returns.[34] Richard did make occasional visits to York, and donated funds for building work on the Minster; his gift is commemorated by a carving of the white hart on a capital of the main arcade, of around 1395. On the feast of Corpus Christi (1 June) in 1396, he attended a large civic reception, where it seems he may have witnessed a special performance of the Corpus Christi or 'mystery' plays, for the chamberlains' accounts list payments for minstrels, decorations and carpentry work, which might refer to the wooden stages or structures required for the plays.[35]

The Corpus Christi plays are the most potent artistic demonstration of civic vitality and community in this period. In contrast with the royal triumphs and entrances staged in London, the mystery-play cycles of York, Coventry, Chester and Wakefield were each produced by the people of the city for themselves, in large part free of direct control from Church or state. They aimed to show the whole of Christian history over the course of a day, in a cycle of short plays or 'pageants' put on by the craft guilds of the city.[36] Each pageant would be staged on a large wagon, hauled through the city from one performance site to the next; audiences would gather at these sites, and see each of the pageants in turn. The guilds were responsible for the whole production and performance of their particular pageant, which they funded by the levy of 'pageant silver', collected from guild members every year. The pageants' themes were often suited to the guild (in ways which seem slightly tasteless to modern eyes) – the Pinners, nail makers, put on the *Play of the Crucifixion*, while the Goldsmiths would show off their finest wares in *Herod and the Magi*.

The audience would see Creation at dawn, and the Last Judgement by torchlight, late at night. The whole of biblical history was spread before the eyes of everyone in the town, with both grandeur and intimacy, acted before small audiences by their friends and colleagues, acquaintances and relatives. And as they watched, in the late fourteenth century, they could see that Judgement was very near – for all of Christian history has already happened; their own time hovers in the dark pause between the *Coronation of Mary* – the penultimate pageant, in which Mary was welcomed bodily into heaven at the end of her earthly life – and the *Last Judgement*. Each person might perceive their own insignificance in comparison with the long span of history. And yet – characteristically of medieval thought – they would also have seen, simultaneously, exactly the reverse. All the significant events of human history were performed by individuals, whether in ignorance or in knowledge; those individuals were just like us, and we like them, and those events reverberate through eternity. One man's lifetime is as nothing to historical time, but one man's soul is infinite, whereas history is finite. In this sense, the awed observer of the Corpus Christi cycle could know that her own soul's fate was of greater importance than a thousand years of history.

These are not really plays for a king. The people of York may have entertained Richard II with their great theatrical achievement as a sign of respect for him, but the plays themselves are resolutely egalitarian, speaking directly to every man and woman of God's providential hand in history, and in their own lives. The tyrannical King Herod rants ineffectually while the Magi, the 'three kings' of the East, quietly submit to the glory of a newborn child.

Of all the cities of his realm, Richard finally placed his greatest hope in his newly declared principality of Chester. By an act of his 1397 parliament he had made it virtually a kingdom within a kingdom; he used the lands seized from the executed Earl of Arundel to increase and enrich the principality, regarding it as a stronghold of his own.[37] He immediately began adding the title 'Prince of Chester' to his royal style. Chester was bound up with his memory of past glory and past wrongs; numerous Cheshiremen who had fought with the Black Prince received pensions from Richard, and in 1398, in the aftermath of his Revenge Parliament, he deposited more than £2,600 at Chester Abbey for distribution to those who had suffered in and after the clash at Radcot Bridge in 1387. It was Cheshiremen Richard relied upon to keep him safe. Yet in the summer of 1399 Chester fell without a fight to Henry Bolingbroke.

This was not because its loyalty to Richard was inadequate or false; rather, it was the outcome of an essentially self-defeating strategy. In his determination to have one place entirely his, entirely loyal, he had alienated the rest of the country; just as he had dismayed Parliament with the promotion of favourites, so he denigrated the rest of his realm to the greater glory of Chester – and the Cheshiremen could not but be outnumbered by the rest of the nation.

Richard himself lacked the spirit to fight alongside his men; he abandoned his own army in the night. The cities he had thought of as his own were lost to him. While he was held prisoner by Bolingbroke in Chester, the aldermen of London came to the city to swear their allegiance to Henry.

Chester's status as a borderland between England and Wales, and as a world unto itself, carried a particular power set apart from the English state. There was a long-lived rumour, still current in the fourteenth century, that King Harold II of England had not been killed at the Battle of Hastings. Instead he was said to have lived out his years anonymously as a holy recluse in Chester, famed for his sanctity.[38] The story would no doubt have appealed to Richard, had he known it.

4
Shrine

I Richard's body have interrèd new;
And on it have bestowed more contrite tears
Than from it issued forcèd drops of blood.
Five hundred poor I have in yearly pay,
Who twice a day their withered hands hold up
Toward heaven to pardon blood;
And I have built two chantries,
Where the sad and solemn priests sing still
For Richard's soul.[1]

On his accession in 1413, Henry V had Richard's body exhumed from the priory at King's Langley, and reinterred at Westminster with great ceremony, in the double tomb Richard had commissioned for Queen Anne and himself upon her death in 1394.[2] The tomb was the last in a series which formed a Plantagenet mausoleum, with the tombs of Edward III, Edward I and Henry III nearby.[3] In the centre of the group was the shrine of Edward the Confessor, whose cult Henry III and Richard had done so much to promote.

This was an age when the dead could speak. Shakespeare has Henry V on his knees the night before the Battle of Agincourt, pleading with God not to use the day's business to punish him for his father's crimes against the deposed king. However long the list of Richard's failings, and however properly Henry IV had been acclaimed by Parliament and people, he had brought about the death of an anointed king, his own lord. The young Henry V's own innocence in the matter was a vital part of chroniclers' adulation for him. A story is told that on hearing of Bolingbroke's invasion, Richard asked the boy, then about twelve and in the king's custody as a hostage, '"Why has your father done this to me? . . . I grieve for your person, in that you will perhaps be deprived of your inheritance because of this unfortunate behaviour of your father."' These were hypocritical words – for Richard had already deprived the boy's father of his inheritance – as well as being disingenuous (or self-deceiving) in their expression of hurt, carrying a barely veiled threat. With great presence of mind, Henry is said to have replied: '"Gracious king and lord, I am truly aggrieved at these rumours, but it is obvious to your lordship, in my estimation, that I am innocent of my father's actions."' This earned him Richard's important declaration that '"I accept that you have no responsibility for that deed"'.[4]

Fear of the dead, and of the providential workings whereby all sins would necessarily be punished, had the corollary of a veneration for the dead. Above all it was the saints whose favour was sought, who could intercede with God on behalf of the sinner, whether living in fear of damnation, or waiting in purgatorial torment. One manuscript now held in the British Library contains a miracle poem about a London saint, written most likely in the 1390s, in the Cheshire dialect. No certain attribution or connection can be adduced for the poem's author, but his Cheshire origins and London subject matter combine two of Richard's greatest associations. The saint was the seventh-century Anglo-Saxon bishop Erkenwald, whose relics had been translated to a shrine east of the high altar in St Paul's in 1148, when Erkenwald was effectively adopted as the patron saint of the city.[5] During Richard's reign his cult was actively promoted by the Bishop of London, Robert Braybrooke, and Richard is likely to have paid his respects to Erkenwald's shrine on several occasions.[6] The poem recounts a miracle performed by Bishop Erkenwald in London during his lifetime. On the conversion of the Anglo-Saxons to Christianity, as the poem explains, pagan temples and structures were taken over and made into churches as a deliberate strategy of persuasion and adaptation, and it opens with just such an excavation and rebuilding project.

Digging down into the foundations of St Paul's, Erkenwald's men find an ornate and beautiful marble tomb, deep buried. They have no idea whose it is or how long it has been there, but the corpse inside is perfectly undamaged as though merely asleep, with all its clothing and accoutrements, including a crown and sceptre, still gleaming. The saint prays to God to provide a solution to this mystery, approaches the corpse, and commands it to speak. The body is suddenly animated by *goste-lyfe*, either a 'ghostly life', or the life force of the Holy Spirit, and he begins to speak. He explains that he lived in London when Brutus had first built the city as 'Troy', five hundred years before Christ, more than a thousand years before the poem's present day. He was a man of law and a judge, set to rule over the city. Erkenwald asks him why he has been buried with the crown and sceptre of a king, and he replies that he was so famed for his justice and impartiality, his uncorruptibility and righteousness, that all the people of the city wished to celebrate him as 'king of wise justice', the greatest Troy had ever seen, or ever would see. But – alas – he lived before Christ, and he cannot be saved without baptism, no matter his virtues. At this the bishop prepares to go and fetch water for baptism, praying that the corpse's animation may last long enough for him to do so, and he says the words of the sacrament, weeping at the man's plight; but then a tear falls upon the body:

With that word that he warpèd, the water of his eyen	*shaped* *eyes*
And tears trillèd adown and on the tomb lighten,	*trickled* *landed*
And one fell on his face, and the freke sighed.	*man*
Then said he with a sadde soun: 'Our Saviour be loved!'[7]	*grave utterance*

The saint's words and his tear have baptized the pagan; with that, the corpse collapses into dust, and his soul is released to heaven.

This poem binds together London's Anglo-Saxon with its supposedly Trojan, British past, and ties both to its fourteenth-century present. The constant work of building and rebuilding the city's churches and palaces was an engagement with time and history, like the collecting and veneration of saints' relics: the past is physically present, in stone and bones, and that presence gives access to an eternity beyond time. More politically, in the context of Richard's reign it is impossible not to note the poem's (albeit ancient) depiction of kingship, as something bestowed on a ruler in recognition of his fitness to rule, his justice and righteousness – and the intimation that 'Troy', London, will not have such a ruler again. But above all the story is about the miraculous power of God and the saints, for whom nothing is impossible.

Saintly intervention was not only sought for the soul. At moments of crisis or trouble, the saints were begged to perform physical miracles to show their favour in this world. The Westminster chronicler describes Richard's going to the shrine of St Edward in the midst of the Great Revolt, the morning of the meeting at Smithfield, to beg for his aid. The saint was well disposed to punish the rebels, he observes, for they had desecrated the shrine by dragging a man out of sanctuary the day before:

> Richard Imworth, steward of the Marshalsea . . . had fled for safety to the church of Westminster and was clinging to the columns of the shrine when he was forcibly dragged away from that holy spot, to be later beheaded, without any judicial process, in the middle of Cheap. But St Edward, to the exaltation of his sainthood and the comfort of the realm, was swift indeed to avenge the wrong offered to him.[8]

Richard wept and prayed at the shrine, surrounded by 'lords, knights, esquires, and countless others' who fervently joined in his supplications. 'Every man, as he rose from prayer, took fresh heart and fresh hope of a happy outcome. Thus inspired, they rode away again', on to Smithfield, and the end of the revolt.[9]

The Westminster chronicler had an obvious interest in celebrating the role of his abbey and its saints, but the bonding and inspiring effects of corporate worship at times of crisis were undoubtedly powerful. In later years Richard may have ceased to exploit such opportunities for public devotion. At the feast of the translation of St Edward in 1390, following his Smithfield tournament, Richard brought his whole chapel entourage to Westminster Abbey for the services of Prime, Vespers and Compline, but during High Mass he sat in the choir wearing his crown, while his queen, also crowned, sat on the north side.[10] The impression is not of collective prayer and devotion, as it had been nine years earlier; rather the king is honouring Westminster Abbey with his royal presence, underlining his distance from his subjects by the ceremony of public crown-wearing.

The Wilton Diptych was made a few years later, around 1395, and it has been argued that this object was effectively a private shrine, an altarpiece for Richard to kneel before in reflection, by which he could direct his meditations towards himself and his kingship.[11] It is oddly representative of Richard's reign as a whole that these decorated panels, surely commissioned by him in precise and elaborate detail, should have proved so difficult to interpret. His kneeling figure is offered support by the royal Anglo-Saxon saints Edmund and Edward, with his chosen patron John the Baptist, who ushers him towards the Christ Child. On the facing panel a red-cross banner echoes both Christ and St George, and recent work has revealed that the orb at the head of the banner contains a miniaturized portrait of an island, presumably representative of England. It seems that Richard is in the act either of rendering the banner up to Christ, or receiving it from him – or both, as a symbolic reference to the idea that he held the throne as a vassal of the Lord. But the angels are painted in surprising attitudes: they all wear the white hart, in iconography which can seem alarmingly hubristic; but some are attentive and gesture towards Richard, while others seem uninvolved, or even engaged in discussions of their own. Richard is not represented in any earthly space, such as the usual chapel or court; rather he kneels in a wasteland, some limbo from which he is granted a view of paradise.[12] The overriding impression for the viewer is of distance, isolation – even self-absorption, despite Richard's pious posture. His exchange with the Christ Child is for ever opaque to us, and we are not permitted to ask.

Reversals of fortune – such as the ignominious end of Wat Tyler – were often attributed to the intervention of the saints, but there are many more direct examples of their miraculous involvement in people's lives. The chroniclers of Richard's reign describe local wonders, such as blood flowing from wood on a martyr's feast day; a young man paralysed and then restored by a saint so that he communicates the vision she has sent him; the healing of a disabled old lady; a drowned girl restored to life; and several instances of a miraculous abundance of corn.[13] They also recount more obviously political events: a vision of Christ's flesh in the Eucharist, disproving the Lollard heresy that the bread did not contain the real presence of Christ; the apparition of an English army, brought by the Virgin Mary, which causes the Scots besieging Carlisle to flee; a reliquary's becoming impossible to carry while near a house of friars (of whom the chronicler sharply disapproved); the uncorrupted and perfectly preserved head of an earl weeks after his controversial execution and the head's exposure on a spike.[14]

Some of the more personal stories are astonishingly moving, as in the account from 1397 of a woman from the village of Tiddington in Warwickshire. She was afflicted with suicidal despair, and tried to hang herself; her husband found her, cut her down and revived her, and for a time she tried to live as normal. Then she was seized once again, and this time the cord she tried to hang herself with broke; instead she threw herself into a lake, trying to drown, but could not succeed. She came to her sister's house, cold and half crazed; her sister tucked her up in bed and went to fetch help. The woman then grabbed a knife and tried to cut out her heart, reaching into the wound and pulling her own entrails from her body – at which terrible, bloody scene her sister and priest arrived, with others. The priest pleaded with her to make her confession, arguing that God had made it so hard for her to kill herself because he wished to save her, for a suicide was eternally damned without confession. At length she began to trust him, and 'confessed in full repentance, received the last sacrament in true faith, and survived for three more hours'. What those hours must have been like for her sister and husband is barely imaginable, but I hope the woman found some sense of peace. The chronicler is utterly sincere in saying that she left behind her 'a great hope for mortal men of God's mercy, which is ever available to those who seek it'.[15]

Richard was himself the witness to a healing miracle in Ely in 1383, when he was sixteen. One of his knights, a close friend named Sir James Berners, was struck by lightning during a violent storm, leaving him dazed and blinded. Richard appealed to the clergy to process to the tomb of St Etheldreda and pray for her intercession for his friend. The knight was led to the altar and received a vision in which he was brought before a judge to be condemned, but was saved by the intervention of Etheldreda and St John the Evangelist – and he recovered his sight and sense completely.[16]

Etheldreda was one of several Anglo-Saxon saints, like Erkenwald, to whom Richard showed great devotion. He certainly visited and supported the shrines of Chad at Lichfield, Winifred at Holywell in Flint, and Edward the Martyr at Wareham.[17] Most important of all were the two chief Anglo-Saxon royal saints Richard had chosen for the Wilton Diptych, Edward the Confessor and Edmund the Martyr. Edmund, martyred by the Vikings in the ninth century and spontaneously venerated by the people soon after his death, had a thriving later medieval cult at Bury, with a great popular following. Edward the Confessor in contrast was a sadly ineffectual, heirless king, sanctified by the efforts of twelfth-century writers on behalf of the crown, and adopted by the Plantagenet kings as the saintly antecessor who had granted the throne to William the Conqueror. Henry III had rebuilt Westminster Abbey in Edward's honour and named his son for the saint, and Richard followed Henry's example, making vast donations to the abbey and supporting its building programmes in his own reign. For both Henry III and Richard II, the appeal of Edward lay in his claims to peace-loving sanctity; he was not associated with martial endeavour, but with a time of peace and stability at the culmination of the Old English royal line, which was then bequeathed to the Normans and their successors. Edward I had looked to King Arthur instead, as a mythical predecessor of heroic warrior stature, while Edward III promoted the cult of St George, an invented paragon of chivalry who rapidly overtook Edward the Confessor in popularity as England's saint.[18] But Richard was devoted to his royal predecessor, and it seems an obvious connection to make that Richard was as interested in Edward's – and Edmund's – royal status as in their sanctity. His sense of history was channelled through the royal line, and he sought glories to burnish that genealogy, while mourning the crises which had broken or besmirched it. His veneration of the Anglo-Saxon kings was of a piece with his attempts to have Edward II canonized, or his famous recitation, while held prisoner in the Tower, of the fallen kings of England.[19]

The royal saints of Anglo-Saxon England were particularly important because England could furnish none after the Conquest; in comparison, France had the towering figure of Louis IX (1214–70), canonized in 1297. But if Richard thought of sanctity and kingship as closely related, he did little to promote his own aura of kingly piety, beyond the iconography of his art and architectural commissions. Indeed he was highly conventional in his public adoration of St Thomas Becket (1120?–70), who was often regarded as a patron of resistance to royal oppression, for he had been martyred in a bitter dispute with Henry II, King of England. Richard took steps to make sure no parallel cult could develop around the corpse of the Earl of Arundel in 1397, having heard that rumour proclaimed him a martyr following his beheading: 'pilgrimages began to be made to his body and miracles declared, amongst other stories that his head, which had been separated from his body, had been miraculously joined to it again'.[20] Richard ordered the body to be exhumed and examined; the head had been sewn on to the body with cord for burial, and he had it torn off again, and the remains reburied in an unmarked site.[21] The hostile chronicler represents this as the vindictive and impious behaviour of a madman, but popular cults could grow with dangerous rapidity, and Richard showed his political nous in preventing it.

Religious belief threatened to take on a dangerous character throughout Richard's reign, through the influence of the Oxford scholar and theologian John Wyclif (d. 1384). His followers became known as 'Lollards', condemned for heresy by the Church and ultimately persecuted, but many of Wyclif's promulgated views were wildly popular and highly influential. At the centre of his reforming critique was a simple equation about Christianity's opposition to worldly wealth; this had a strong basis in scripture, and was a recurring problem for the medieval Church: Christ had embraced poverty, and so it was argued that the Church must be poor. Wyclif declared that all material wealth belonged by definition to the state and laity, not the Church, and that in holding and hoarding wealth the clergy were necessarily in a state of sin, and were therefore unworthy of their office. In moderate form these ideas were useful to the crown and government, and in the later years of Edward III's reign and the beginning of Richard's Wyclif was asked more than once to produce legal arguments to justify the crown's right to appropriate Church property at times of need.[22] John of Gaunt was for some years Wyclif's patron and supporter, and there was a faction at Richard's court known as the 'Lollard knights', all of whom to some degree adhered to his views.[23]

But the situation was delicate, and rapidly Wyclif's teachings became more controversial. His understanding of the Church as a whole created a dramatic challenge to papal and episcopal authority. Wyclif believed in predestination, by which some were saved and some damned, unknowably during this life, but irreversibly. The only true 'Church' was that composed of the elect, those who are saved – and there is no way of knowing whether any cleric, up to and including the pope, is saved or damned. Furthermore, all authority in this world comes directly from God, and can justly be held only by the righteous, who are in a state of grace. Any priest who sins, therefore, has no right to his office; and because civil power and dominion is inherently flawed and sinful, the clergy should have no part in it: 'temporality and spirituality be two parts of Holy Church, and therefore he that taketh him to the one should not meddle him with the other . . . all manner of curates both high and low be fully excused of temporal office'.[24] It followed that for Wyclif the reformation of the Church would require the restoration of all its wealth and property, and all secular jurisdiction, to the secular state and the laity.

Clerical chroniclers fill their accounts of these arguments with venom, and cite papal condemnation of Wyclif's writings in great detail. They immediately connected Wyclif's teachings to the Great Revolt of 1381, and once the association of Lollardy with sedition was accepted by those in power, support for Lollardy noticeably drained away in court and Parliament. But the penetration of Wyclif's arguments throughout society is unmistakable, as is the serious moral character of many of the 1381 rebels' complaints. William Langland's inspirational poem *Piers Plowman* is a visionary social commentary and critique, fired by the urgent necessity of every man's seeking his own salvation, while society stands on the brink of destruction. The leaders of the Revolt made open reference to the poem in their letters and broadsides.[25] Langland wrote and rewrote it during the 1370s and 1380s, and the dating of each version is a complex task. It has long been thought that he responded to the use of his work in the Revolt by producing the much-edited, more elliptical 'C' text of the poem, which contrasts with the sometimes almost revolutionary fervour of the earlier 'B' text. But whether the latter was written before 1381 and proved to be, in part, incendiary, or was written afterwards as a bitter reflection on the causes of the uprising,[26] Langland echoes Wyclif at his most extreme, in a popular work widely known throughout England in the period, with more than sixty manuscripts surviving to this day. He declares that the 'Donation of Constantine', by which the first Christian emperor of Rome endowed the Church, was the fatal moment of destruction:

If knighthood and kind wit, and the commons and conscience	*common sense*
Together love loyally, believe it well, ye bishops –	
The lordship of lands lose ye shall for ever,	
And live as *Levitici*, as Our Lord you teacheth:	*Levites*
Per primicias et decimas . . .	*By first-fruits and tithes*
When Constantine of courtesy Holy Church endowed	
With lands and ledes, lordship and rents,	*properties*
An angel men heard on high at Rome cry:	
"*Dos ecclesie* this day hath drunken venom,	*Endowment of the Church*
And those that have Peter's power are poisoned all!"	
A medicine must thereto that may amend prelates,	

That should pray for the peace;
possession them letteth. *binds, hinders*
Taketh their lands, ye lords, and
let them live by dymes; *tithes*
If possession be poison, and
imperfect them make,
Good were to discharge them for
Holy Church's sake,
And purge them of poison, ere
more peril fall.[27]

This echoes the recorded words of one of Wyclif's staunchest followers, Nicholas of Hereford. In May 1382 he preached in English to an appreciative crowd in St Frideswide's churchyard, Oxford. Criticizing the wealth of the Church in its entirety, he went on to say that all clerics with temporal possessions should be disinherited, and that rather than oppressing the common people with taxes, the king should confiscate the Church's property. He ended by encouraging the laity to seize the Church's property themselves if the king did not.[28]

Nicholas of Hereford's career is good evidence of the power of a Lollard faction at court. Sir William Neville was in royal service as a knight of the chamber, and while Hereford was imprisoned for heresy in Nottingham Castle between 1387 and 1391, Neville used his influence to protect him, apparently providing him with books and possibly even disseminating his writings.[29] His fate would have been somewhat different during the reign of Henry IV, just as the passage quoted from *Piers Plowman* above could not safely have been written a few years later.

Despite the Lollard sympathizers at his court, Richard's own views on Lollardy seem to have been conventionally orthodox, following the prevailing tide of increasing condemnation in the aftermath of the Great Revolt. Nevertheless, his personal involvement cannot be assumed for the first half of the reign. Richard was still only fifteen when the Archbishop of Canterbury petitioned Parliament in 1382 for greater powers against heretics, which were granted.[30] The Merciless Parliament of 1388 was also concerned with the problem of heretical writings and preaching,[31] but Richard's role in that parliament was no more than that of a figurehead – and indeed clerical observers continued to express worries about the influence of pro-Lollard magnates on Parliament.

However, in 1388 the king's council began to move against suspected heretics among the aristocracy, summoning Sir Thomas Latimer (a soldier who had served with the Black Prince, and attended upon Joan, Richard II's mother, until her death in 1385) to appear before them with his books, which were alleged to be counter to orthodoxy.[32] Such investigations continued during Richard's majority, and in 1395 a number of heretics took an oath before chancery, abjuring Lollardy 'on penalty of being punished with the forfeiture of all their goods to the king without further process of law'.[33] In the same year, despite being absent in Ireland, Richard responded rapidly to the news that Lollard sympathizers had nailed a manifesto to the doors of Westminster Hall. The chronicler tells us that he made one of his Lollard knights, Sir Richard Stury, swear to abjure the heresy, on pain of death if he should go back on his oath.[34] One of his household squires was similarly made to renounce his heretical views before the king at Windsor in August, when he took an oath never to read any Lollard books in English or to have any such in his house.[35] The Dominican Roger Dymock presented Richard with an illuminated copy of his anti-Lollard *Treatise Against the Twelve Errors* around this time; on the opening folio Richard is depicted enthroned in miniature, and his arms and white hart symbol form the page's decorated borders.[36] Two years later, in March 1397, Richard ordered Sir William Scrope to bring all the heretical prisoners in his custody before the king for personal examination.[37]

Historians have drawn on these actions in attributing to Richard a personal drive against heresy, epitomized in the praise for his destruction of heretics which is inscribed on his tomb in a striking epitaph. But I suspect that his stern response to Lollardy was no more than another facet of his obsession with the obedience of his subjects. In the broader context of the rather confused and confusing epitaph (no one knows why Richard should have chosen to compare himself to Homer), the relevant phrase is both more conventional, as all rulers promise to protect the Church, and more open to ambiguous interpretation, melding divinity with kingship:

> He was truthful in discourse and full of reason. Tall in body, he was prudent in mind as Homer. He favoured the Church; he overthrew the proud and threw down whoever

> violated the royal prerogative. He crushed heretics and laid low their friends.[38]

Richard may have believed himself an opponent of heresy, but he took no real measures against that close group of his knights who seem to have been at least protectors, and perhaps promulgators, of the Lollard heresy and Wyclif's ideas.[39] Despite papal condemnation and his expulsion from Oxford University in 1382, Wyclif himself was permitted to withdraw to private life in Lutterworth, where he continued to write until his death two years later. Yet if Richard was initially attracted to Wyclif's teaching for its emphasis on the power of worldly kingship and the king's right to all property of the Church, Lollard condemnation of shrines, relics and images as near-idolatry was in little sympathy with Richard's style of piety. Furthermore, the ascetic Lollard attack on pride and extravagance would hardly have appealed to him: 'the multitude of crafts not needful . . . nourisheth much sin in waste, curiosity and disguising . . . goldsmiths and armourers and all manner crafts not needful to man . . . should be destroyed for the increase of virtue'.[40] Richard's statements about heresy gain venom in his later years, but they continue to betray an overriding interest in his rule and his subjects' obedience. In a letter to the Bishop of Chichester he wrote of 'damnable errors repugnant to the faith . . . which would bring ruin to the diocese if not resisted by the arm of the king's majesty'; he feared that such heresies would 'infect the people of the whole realm, the ruling whereof is committed to the king from on high'.[41] Richard's own interests in these debates were perhaps satisfied merely by the Lollards', as all his subjects', immediate obedience to his will.

Lollardy is chiefly and justly remembered now for inspiring the translation of the Bible into English, and its rapid distribution among the laity. Around 250 copies of the Wycliffite Bible survive, their original owners from all classes of society, which only makes it more difficult to credit the horror – and hauteur – with which this was greeted by one of the chroniclers of Richard's reign:

> The Gospel, which Christ gave to the clergy and the doctors of the church, that they might administer it to the laity and to weaker brethren, according to the demands of the time and the needs of the individual, as a sweet food for the mind, that Master John Wyclif translated from Latin into the language not of angels but of Englishmen, so that he made that common and open to the laity, and to women who were able to read, which used to be for literate and perceptive clerks, and spread the Evangelists' pearls to be trampled by swine. And thus that which was dear to the clergy and the laity alike became as it were a jest common to both, and the clerk's jewels became the playthings of laymen, that the laity might enjoy now forever what had once been the clergy's talent from on high.[42]

This chronicler believed that these events must presage the end of the world. His 'not . . . angels but . . . Englishmen' is a bitter reversal of Bede's famous story of the origins of the conversion of the Anglo-Saxons to Christianity. The pope, seeing for the first time some fair-haired Anglo-Saxon slaves, is said to have commented that they were 'non Angli sed angeli' ('not English but angels'), and so he sent Augustine on his mission to convert this people. Now, the fourteenth-century chronicler implies with his mirrored reference, all those centuries of faith are about to be lost, scripture made useless. French translations of the Bible had long been widely available in England, and were valuable, often highly illuminated possessions: but they were of course the property of the aristocracy; Richard himself had purchased one when he was thirteen.[43] It was not the act of translation into a vernacular which aroused such fire; it was the seditious offering to the common people of the right to their own interpretation of scripture, and hence their own moral judgement on their betters. As such, it is perhaps not surprising that so many manuscripts of the Wycliffite Bible should be expensively illuminated and professionally produced. Copies are known to have belonged to aristocrats, and even to kings Henry IV, VI and VII: scripture had always been thought to be safe in the hands of the ruling classes.[44]

It is not known whether Wyclif himself was actually involved at any stage in the English Bible translation, which was a major undertaking.[45] The 'General Prologue' to the English Bible, written probably in the 1390s towards the end of the great project, mentions 'diverse fellows and helpers' and four, complex stages to the work of reinterpreting an authoritative Vulgate text in the English vernacular.[46] The sheer, scholarly attention paid to the English language and to the act of translation itself in this work is one of its greatest gifts to the time, and it seems unlikely to be accidental that this project coincided with such a general flowering of literature in English. Chaucer's works are the most well known to modern readers, but the anonymous authors of this period produced texts of outstanding creativity and beauty, often preserved in single manuscripts.

The author of the great romance *Sir Gawain and the Green Knight* also wrote a dream vision of paradise, seen through the grieving eyes of a father who has lost his infant daughter: *Pearl*. The Dreamer speaks of his lost Pearl, his jewel, now horribly buried in mud and earth. Falling asleep, he enters an impossible landscape of dazzling beauty – trees with silver leaves, crystal cliffs, the gravel in the river made of precious stones, golden fruit in the trees, brightly coloured birds in the air. Then he sees a maiden dressed all in white, decked with pearls, whom he recognizes as his lost pearl, his daughter. He addresses her with love-longing and yearning, and she replies with stern religious instruction: he must understand that she is not his pearl, but God's, and that she is now in heaven among the blessed. She explains to him the infinite grace of heaven, which renders earthly understanding meaningless:

The court of the kingdom of God	
alive	*living*
Has a property in itself being:	*of its own nature*
All that may therein arrive	

Of all the realm is queen or king,	
And never other yet shall deprive,	*never yet take from another*
But each one fain of other's having	*joyous for what the other has*
And would their crowns were worth those five	*five times more*
If possible were their mending.[47]	*improvement*

These are the economics of infinity, of heaven, untainted by the scarcity of earthly life, by which one man's possessions cannot be another's, and one's gain is another's loss. The explanation is transcendant – and yet the humanity of this poem is remarkable. The Dreamer is not released from his grief; instead he is enabled to express it, at anguished length, to his dead daughter, and to receive in return some sense of the eternal truth which lies beyond earthly suffering, beyond our reach and understanding. At the poem's end he returns to the world, with a pearl of faith to surround the grit of his suffering: but the faith required the suffering, and requires it still.

The fourteenth century was a great era of visionary writing, inspirational of and inspired by the growth and intensity of lay piety associated with Lollards and orthodox thought alike. Julian of Norwich (1342–*c.*1416), an anchorite – a hermit physically walled up in her cell, dedicated to prayer – received some visions from God during her sickness in 1372. Over the following twenty years, she wrote up her visions in English and interpreted them for others, offering the wisdom which God had brought to her. In one of her most famous images she receives a revelation about the nature of the whole created universe:

> He showed a little thing, the quantity of a hazelnut in the palm of my hand, and it was as round as a ball. I looked thereupon with the eye of my understanding and thought: 'What may this be?' And it was generally answered thus: 'It is all that is made.' I marvelled how it might last, for methought it might suddenly have fallen to nought for little. And I was answered in my understanding: 'It lasteth and ever shall, for God loveth it.'

God's love is the defining quality which animates and keeps all reality, for Julian; she observes that looking for fulfilment to the little ball of creation, rather than to the love of the creator without whom it cannot exist, is to mistake nothing for something:

> For this is the cause why we be not all in ease of heart and soul: for we seek here rest in these things that are so little, wherein is no rest, and know not our God that is almighty, all wise, all good; for he is the very rest.[48]

Richard visited a London anchorite in 1381, and made donations to support anchorites in various towns during his reign. But his devotion seems to have been resolutely of a practical sort: he prayed for favour, for intervention, for mastery over his enemies and the love and submission of his people – for all 'these things that are so little', which brought him no rest.[49] Not for Richard the heaven where all who enter are queens and kings; his lone regality, carried in royal blood and in anointing, was his access to the divine.

In 1388 Richard presented the shrine of Edward the Confessor with a valuable gold and ruby ring, on unusual terms: when he was in the country he was to retain use of the ring for his lifetime, but when he left the realm and on his death, it would be returned to St Edward. Apparently he failed to keep his own contract in 1399 when he went to Ireland, for the ring was eventually returned to the shrine by Henry V after 1413.[50] But the agreement itself is revealing of Richard's sense of his relationship with, and likeness to, his holy antecessor. When Richard is in his and Edward's kingdom, he suggests, the bond between them is such that his ownership of the ring is commensurate with Edward's possession of it. Edward's own chief miracle story, in honour of which he is depicted holding a ring on the Wilton Diptych, was that finding he had no coins to hand, he gave away a valuable ring from his finger to a poor beggar. The beggar is later revealed to be John the Evangelist, and he returns the ring to the king with his blessing, and the promise that they will be peers in heaven.[51] In presenting Edward with a ring, therefore, and in keeping it with him as a 'gift' from Edward, Richard sought to associate himself closely with the saint and with his miracles.

There is something painfully appropriate in the regard of Richard II for Edward the Confessor. Edward's cult was invented and sustained by and for kings, for their own purposes, and it never mustered real popular support or a groundswell of feeling. It was a literary and artistic cult created by patronage, without the widespread faith or veneration necessary to inspire love and loyalty. Edward's tomb at Westminster Abbey was designed as a glorious shrine to the sanctity of kingship, of a kind that, in his own time, only Richard II believed in.

5
Epilogue

I had pity of his passion that prince was of Wales, — *suffering*
And eke our crowned king, til Christ wills no longer. — *also*
And as a liege to his lord, though I little had,
All my whole heart was his while he in health reigned.[1]

The early fifteenth-century English poem *Richard the Redeless* ('Richard the Counsel-less') captures in the midst of its stern criticisms the essential difficulty of betraying an anointed king. Subjects had a duty to love their king, as these lines sorrowfully demonstrate. In 1402 Henry IV faced a group of friars whom he suspected of stirring up rebellion with the rumour that Richard still lived. It had not taken long for dissatisfaction with Henry's rule to encourage nostalgia for Richard, and all the difficulties of Henry's reign could be interpreted as judgements upon him for Richard's deposition and death. The chronicler's description of the king's interrogation of the friars is startlingly vivid.

> 'Tell me truth as it is in thy heart: if thou sawest King Richard and me in a field fighting together, with whom wouldst thou stand?' 'Forsooth,' said the friar, 'with him, for I am more beholden to him.' Then said the king unto him, 'Thou wouldst that I and all the lords of my realm were dead?' The friar said, 'Nay.' 'What wouldst thou do with me,' said the king, 'if thou hadst the victory over me?' The friar said, 'I would make you the duke of Lancaster.' 'Thou art not my friend,' said the king, 'and therefore thou shalt lose thine head.'[2]

The friar's damning final statement, that he would remake Henry as the duke he should be, carries a dreadful weight of righteousness, and Henry's response is merely tyrannous. He sought to build a case by which the friars could properly be charged with treason, and promptly received word of a conspiracy: that five hundred men had agreed to gather on Oxford plain on Midsummer Eve, to go in search of King Richard, and that prophecies had told them that the former king would return and defeat his rival. Henry questions the apparent ringleader, the friars' master, asking him whether he believes that Richard is alive:

> 'I say not that he liveth, but I say if he lives, he is true King of England.' The king said, 'He resigned.' The master answered, 'He resigned against his will in prison, the which is not in the law.' The king answered, 'He resigned with his good will.' 'He would not have resigned,' said the master, 'if he had been at his freedom; and a resignation made in prison is not free.' Then said the king, 'He was deposed.' The master answered, 'When he was king he was taken by

> force, and put into prison, and despoiled of his realm, and you have usurped the crown.' The king said, 'I have not usurped the crown, but I was chosen thereto by election.' The master answered, 'The election is naught, living the true and lawful possessor; and if he be dead, he is dead by you, and if he be dead by you, you have lost all the right and title that ye might have to the crown.' Then said the king to him, 'By my head you shall lose your head.'[3]

There was no reasoning that could adequately eradicate the paradoxes of Henry's situation; the friars were hanged at Tyburn and then beheaded. According to the chronicler, Henry had to convene three different juries before he found one that would pronounce sentence of guilt, and the jurors later came to the friars' fellows to beg forgiveness, explaining that they had been in fear of their lives.

Richard had not been the king the country had wanted or needed, but he was incontrovertibly the rightful king by custom and descent, and once dead, he was a much more potent focus for political loyalty. In appropriating Richard's cause, the rebels against Henry IV used him as a figure of true kingship, evacuated of the individuality which had caused his downfall – represented him, in fact, as Richard had always represented himself. It is an irony that his deposition had indeed turned on personality, on his subjects' impressions of his character. One of the articles of his impeachment in Parliament stated the case directly:

> Also, the same king was accustomed almost continually to be so changeable and dissembling in his words and writings,

> and altogether contrary to himself . . . that almost no living person who knew what sort of person he was, could or wished to trust him. Rather he was thought to be so untrustworthy and inconstant that it became a disgrace, not only to his person, but also to his whole realm.[4]

It seems that Richard's mind was opaque to his subjects, his unpredictability intolerable. But what is most revealing is the critical importance not of Richard's actual nature – which was and remains inaccessible – but of the image of the king: '*he was thought* to be so untrustworthy', *reputatur* in the Latin. Being thought to be untrustworthy is no better – indeed in political terms much worse – than actually being untrustworthy. Richard died as he had lived, by the image he projected of himself. More directly, Archbishop Arundel is said to have pointed out Richard's paradoxes to his handsome face: 'Thou art a fair man, but thou art the falsest of men'; at the end of this diatribe against Richard's crimes, 'the king knew not what he should say'.[5] As we approach him through contemporary records and chronicles, any sense of the 'real' man beneath the image recedes, never to be caught. Chroniclers tell us what they think he said or did, or that bias or rumour believed he had done or said – and even then they give us a Richard who baffled those around him. But the idea of Richard II is as real an object of historical study as the man himself. When it comes to trying to understand the fate of a king, the idea of him may be the only real object of study there is.

Notes

When quoting from primary sources, I have usually followed the published translations of French and Latin where they are available. Where I have given my own translation instead – or where I have modernized Middle English spelling – this is indicated in the relevant note, or at first mention for a text that is repeatedly quoted. Glosses and translations accompanying verse extracts are my own.

ABBREVIATIONS

AC	*The Anonimalle Chronicle*, ed. V. H. Galbraith (Manchester: Manchester University Press, 1927)
Brut	*The Brut, or The Chronicles of England, Part II*, ed. Friedrich W. D. Brie (London: Early English Text Society, 1908)
Chaucer Multitext	*The Multitext Edition: The Norman Blake Editions of The Canterbury Tales*, ed. Estelle Stubbs, Michael Pidd, Orietta Da Rold, Simon Horobin and Claire Thomson with Linda Cross (Sheffield: University of Sheffield, 2013); http://www.chaucermss.org/multitext, accessed 25 April 2015
Complete Shakespeare	*The Complete Pelican Shakespeare*, ed. Stephen Orgel and A. R. Braunmuller (Harmondsworth: Penguin, 2002)
Concordia	Richard Maidstone, *Concordia: The Reconciliation of Richard II with London*, ed. David R. Carlson and trans. A. G. Rigg (Kalamazoo, Mich.: Western Michigan University, 2004)
CR	*Chronicles of the Revolution, 1397–1400*, trans. C. Given-Wilson (Manchester: Manchester University Press, 1993)
CTM	*Chronicque de la traïson et mort de Richart Deux roy d'Engleterre*, ed. and trans. Benjamin Williams (London: S. & J. Bentley, Wilson & Fley, 1846)
EHD	*English Historical Documents: Volume IV: 1327–1485*, ed. A. R. Myers (London: Eyre & Spottiswoode, 1969)
EngC	*An English Chronicle 1377–1461: A New Edition*, ed. William Marx (Woodbridge: Boydell Press, 2003)
Eulogium	*Eulogium (Historiarum sive Temporis): Chronicon ab Orbe Condito Usque ad Annum Domini M.CCC.LXCI*, ed. Frank Scott Haydon, 3 vols (London: Longman, 1858–63)

Foedera	*Foedera, Conventiones, Literæ, et Cujuscunque Generis Acta Publica*, ed. Thomas Rymer, 17 vols (London: J. Tonson, 1726–35)
Froissart	*The Online Froissart*, ed. Peter Ainsworth and Godfried Croenen, version 1.5 (Sheffield: HRIOnline, 2013); http://www.hrionline.ac.uk/onlinefroissart, accessed 30 March 2015
KC	*Knighton's Chronicle, 1337–1396*, ed. and trans. G. H. Martin (Oxford: Oxford University Press, 1995)
Manere	*La Manere de la renonciatione del Roy Richard de sa corone*, ed. G. O. Sayles, in 'The Manner of King Richard's Renunciation: A "Lancastrian Narrative"?', *Bulletin of the Institute of Historical Research* 54 (1981), pp. 257–70
Memorials	*Memorials of London and London Life in the 13th, 14th and 15th Centuries*, ed. H. T. Riley (London: Longmans, Green, 1868); http://www.british-history.ac.uk/no-series/memorials-london-life/, accessed 1 April 2015
ODNB	*Oxford Dictionary of National Biography* (Oxford: Oxford University Press, 2004); http://www.oxforddnb.com
PROME	*Parliament Rolls of Medieval England*, ed. C. Given-Wilson et al. (Leicester: Scholarly Digital Editions, 2005); http://www.sd-editions.com/PROME, accessed 30 March 2015
Regal Image	*The Regal Image of Richard II and the Wilton Diptych*, ed. Dillian Gordon, Lisa Monnas and Caroline Elam (London: Harvey Miller, 1997)
Saul	Nigel Saul, *Richard II* (New Haven, Conn.: Yale University Press, 1997)
StAC	*The St Albans Chronicle: The* Chronica Maiora *of Thomas of Walsingham*, ed. and trans. John Taylor, Wendy R. Childs and Leslie Watkiss, 2 vols (Oxford: Clarendon Press, 2003–11)
Usk	*The Chronicle of Adam Usk*, ed. and trans. C. Given-Wilson (Oxford: Clarendon Press, 1997)
VRS	*Historia Vitae et Regni Ricardi Secundi*, ed. George B. Stow, Jr (Philadelphia, Penn.: University of Pennsylvania Press, 1977)
WC	*Westminster Chronicle, 1381–1394*, ed. and trans. L. C. Hector and Barbara F. Harvey (Oxford: Clarendon Press, 1982)

PROLOGUE

1. *The Tragedy of King Richard the Second*, ed. Frances E. Dolan, in *Complete Shakespeare*, p. 991 (IV.i.279–89).
2. *AC*, pp. 107–10; *StAC*, I, pp. 136–40.
3. *StAC*, II, p. 216.
4. *Manere*, p. 267.
5. *Richard the Second*, ed. Dolan, in *Complete Shakespeare*, p. 991 (IV.i.279–89).

6. *An English Chronicle of the Reigns of Richard II, Henry IV, Henry V, and Henry VI, 1377–1461*, ed. J. S. Davies (London: Longman, 1856), p. 12 (modernized by LA; reading preferred to *EngC*, p. 20).
7. *StAC*, I, p. 36.
8. *EHD*, p. 122.
9. *EngC*, p. 24 (spelling modernized by LA); *Eulogium*, III, p. 383.

1. PARLIAMENT

1. *The Tragedy of King Richard the Second*, ed. Frances E. Dolan, in *Complete Shakespeare*, p. 990 (IV.i.228–9).
2. Usk, p. 63.
3. Usk, p. 65.
4. For discussion of similar matters, see Paul Strohm, *Hochon's Arrow: The Social Imagination of Fourteenth-Century Texts* (Princeton, NJ: Princeton University Press, 1992), especially the introduction at pp. 3–9.
5. *StAC*, I, pp. 814, 848; Richard II: Parliament of January 1397, item 14, in *PROME*.
6. *Concordia*, lines 112, 130–41, 455–62.
7. M. P. Meyer, M. M. Meyer and S. Luce, 'L'Entrevue d'Ardres, 1396', *Annuaire-bulletin de la Société de l'histoire de France*, 18 (1881), pp. 209–24, at pp. 211–14, 217; *StAC*, II, p. 47.
8. The National Archives currency converter (www.nationalarchives.gov.uk/currency/) gives a figure of nearly £230,000 (as in 2005) for £470 in 1390, and more than £1.5 million for £3,300 – but in 1390 a house could be rented in the city of London for £2–3 a year, which by the same scale is only £1,200 in 2005 prices; relative purchasing power makes all comparisons difficult.
9. Meyer et al., 'L'Entrevue d'Ardres', pp. 211–17 (trans. LA).
10. *WC*, p. 139.
11. *WC*, pp. 161–3. These claims are echoed elsewhere: *StAC*, I, pp. 620–25.
12. *WC*, p. 163.
13. *VRS*, p. 156, trans. in *CR*, p. 130.
14. *StAC*, I, pp. 621–3.
15. *KC*, p. 354.
16. *KC*, p. 357.
17. *KC*, pp. 360–61.
18. *KC*, p. 369.
19. Richard II: Parliament of October 1386, item 20, trans. C. Given-Wilson, in *PROME*.
20. *KC*, pp. 369–71.
21. *StAC*, I, pp. 824–7.
22. *KC*, p. 393.
23. *KC*, pp. 395–7.
24. *KC*, p. 395.
25. See John L. Leland, 'Bealknap, Sir Robert (d. 1401)', *ODNB*.
26. *WC*, pp. 206–8.
27. *KC*, p. 407.

28. *StAC*, I, pp. 838–41; *KC*, pp. 418–25; *WC*, pp. 220–25.
29. See John L. Leland, 'Tresilian, Sir Robert (d. 1388)', *ODNB*.
30. Richard II: Parliament of February 1388, item 9, in *PROME*.
31. See John L. Leland, 'Burley, Sir Simon (1336?–1388)', *ODNB*.
32. Richard II: Parliament of February 1388 (following Easter adjournment), item 16, in *PROME*.
33. *WC*, pp. 390–92; *StAC*, I, pp. 864–6; *KC*, pp. 528–30.
34. *StAC*, I, p. 866.
35. *KC*, p. 531.
36. Saul, p. 323.
37. *VRS*, p. 134; Usk, p. 18. For time spent at Sheen 1377–94, see the itinerary in Saul, pp. 469–72.
38. *StAC*, I, pp. 960–62, printed from BL MS Cotton Faustina B.IX. The story does not appear in other chronicle traditions, but is also present in abbreviated form in Corpus Christi College, Cambridge MS 7, fol. 69v[a], written before 1400, which states that Richard polluted the Abbey with the earl's blood.
39. *StAC*, II, p. 30.
40. Saul, pp. 277–81.
41. Usk, p. 19.
42. Usk, pp. 18–20.
43. 800,000 francs: Saul, p. 228.
44. Richard II: Parliament of January 1397, item 28, in *PROME*.
45. *StAC*, II, p. 60; D. M. Bueno de Mesquita, 'The Foreign Policy of Richard II in 1397: Some Italian Letters', *English Historical Review* 56 (1941), pp. 628–36, at p. 633.
46. Richard II: Parliament of January 1397, item 14, trans. C. Given-Wilson, in *PROME*.
47. Ibid., item 15.
48. *StAC*, II, pp. 64–72.
49. Richard II: Parliament of September 1397, opening, trans. C. Given-Wilson, in *PROME*.
50. *StAC*, II, pp. 76–8; *VRS*, p. 140, trans. in *CR*, p. 57.
51. Richard II: Parliament of September 1397, item 11, trans. C. Given-Wilson, in *PROME*.
52. Ibid., item 13.
53. Usk, p. 29.
54. Usk, pp. 28–31; *VRS*, p. 143, trans. in *CR*, p. 59.
55. *CR*, p. 96.
56. 'Concerning Thomas duke of Gloucester': Richard II: Pleas of the Crown before the Parliament of September 1397, trans. C. Given-Wilson, in *PROME*.
57. Anthony Tuck, 'Thomas [Thomas of Woodstock], duke of Gloucester (1355–1397)', *ODNB*.
58. 'Concerning Thomas duke of Gloucester' (spelling modernized by LA).
59. 'Concerning Thomas earl of Warwick': Richard II: Pleas of the Crown before the Parliament of September 1397, in *PROME*.
60. C. Given-Wilson, 'Mowbray, Thomas (I) (1366–1399)', *ODNB*.
61. William Stubbs, *The Constitutional History of England: Its Origins and Development*, 3 vols, 6th edn (Oxford: Clarendon Press, 1903–6), II, pp. 522–3.
62. 'The judgments touching the dukes of Hereford and Norfolk': Richard II: Pleas of the Crown before the Parliament of September 1397 (trans. LA), in *PROME*. Cf. *VRS*, p. 149, trans. in *CR*, pp. 62–3.

63. *CTM*, pp. 14–17.
64. *StAC*, II, p. 108; *CTM*, pp. 21–2.
65. Saul, pp. 288–9.
66. *CR*, p. 147.
67. Usk, pp. 58–60; *StAC*, II, pp. 150–56.
68. The Roll awkwardly explains in an aside: '(on which day King Richard, the second since the conquest, had summoned his parliament to be held there; which summons was of no force or effect, because of the acceptance of the renunciation made by the said King Richard, and of the deposition of the same King Richard, which took place on the same Tuesday, as appears more fully from the record and process of this made and enrolled on this roll of parliament)': Henry IV: Parliament of October 1399, item 1, trans. C. Given-Wilson, in *PROME*.
69. Ibid., item 2.
70. *The Great Chronicle of London*, ed. A. H. Thomas and I. D. Thornley (Gloucester: Alan Sutton, 1983), p. 76 (spelling modernized and some words translated by LA).

2. BATTLEFIELD

1. *Life of the Black Prince, by the Herald of Sir John Chandos*, ed. Mildred K. Pope and Eleanor C. Lodge (Oxford: Clarendon Press, 1910), lines 1598–630 (translation modernized by LA).
2. Gervase Mathew, *The Court of Richard II* (London: John Murray, 1968), pp. 22–3.
3. *Sir Gawain and the Green Knight*, lines 37–53: British Library MS Cotton Nero A.x, fol. 91v (punctuation and capitalization are editorial; obsolete letter forms modernized by LA).
4. See W. Mark Ormrod, *Edward III* (New Haven, Conn.: Yale University Press, 2011), pp. 498–523.
5. *AC*, p. 90.
6. John Clanvowe, *The Two Ways*, in *The Works of Sir John Clanvowe*, ed. V. J. Scattergood (Cambridge: D. S. Brewer, 1975), pp. 57–80, at pp. 69–70 (spelling modernized and some words translated by LA).
7. Richard II: Parliament of October 1377, item 16 (trans. LA), in *PROME*.
8. Richard W. Kaeuper, *War, Justice, and Public Order: England and France in the Later Middle Ages* (Oxford: Clarendon Press, 1988), pp. 353–6.
9. *VRS*, p. 62 (trans. LA).
10. *KC*, pp. 222–4 (spelling modernized and some words translated by LA).
11. *AC*, p. 134.
12. Court of King's Bench (KB145/3/6/1), cited in Saul, p. 62.
13. *AC*, p. 139 (trans. LA).
14. *KC*, p. 214; see also *StAC*, p. 418.
15. *AC*, pp. 142–3. On the chronicler's likely identity and status as eyewitness, see the references given by Saul, p. 65, n. 39.
16. Froissart: Besançon, Bibliothèque Municipale, MS 865, fols. 73v–74r.

17. Caroline M. Barron, 'Richard II and London', in *Richard II: The Art of Kingship*, ed. Anthony Goodman and James Gillespie (Oxford: Clarendon Press, 1999), pp. 129–54, at p. 141.
18. *EHD*, pp. 174–5.
19. *EHD*, pp. 142–3.
20. *StAC*, I, p. 514.
21. Cambridge, University Library MS Dd.14.2, fol. 312r, quoted in Steven Justice, *Writing and Rebellion: England in 1381* (Berkeley, Calif.: University of California Press, 1994), p. 251 (obsolete letter forms modernized and punctuation added by LA).
22. Froissart: Besançon, Bibliothèque Municipale, MS 865, fol. 79v.
23. See J. J. N. Palmer, 'The Last Summons of the Feudal Army in England (1385)', *English Historical Review* 83 (1968), pp. 771–5.
24. *StAC*, I, pp. 762–4; *WC*, pp. 128–30; Froissart: Besançon MS 865, fol. 191r.
25. *KC*, p. 336; cf. *StAC*, I, p. 764.
26. Richard II: Parliament of October 1385, item 14, trans. C. Given-Wilson, in *PROME*.
27. Ibid., item 17.
28. See Anthony Tuck, 'Vere, Robert de (1362–1392)', *ODNB*.
29. *Brut*, p. 343.
30. One chronicler says that he 'won the prize for the first day' (*WC*, p. 450), but Froissart describes it in detail, names a French lord as the first day's winner, and does not mention Richard's competing. There are no other references to his direct participation in tournaments.
31. *Brut*, p. 343 (spelling modernized and some words translated by LA). Cf. *EngC*, p. 12. Froissart says the procession was of sixty knights and ladies, leading with silver chains: Harley MS 4379–4380, fol. 101r.
32. Noted as first used here in the contemporary account of *VRS*, p. 132.
33. *Foedera*, VIII, p. 75.
34. See C. Given-Wilson, 'Richard II and the Higher Nobility', in *Richard II: The Art of Kingship*, ed. Goodman and Gillespie, pp. 107–28, at pp. 123–7.
35. Statute on livery and maintenance, 1390: *EHD*, p. 1116.
36. Saul, pp. 393–4.
37. *Richard the Redeless*, in *Richard the Redeless and Mum the Sothsegger*, ed. James M. Dean (Kalamazoo, Mich.: University of Western Michigan, 2000), lines 32–50 (spelling modernized by LA).
38. Philippe de Mézières, *Epistre au roi Richart: Letter to King Richard II*, ed. and trans. G. W. Coopland (Liverpool: Liverpool University Press, 1975), pp. 124–6 (trans. LA).
39. British Library MS Royal 20.B.vi.

3. CITY

1. *diapered*: Decorated or ornamented with repeated patterns.
2. *Wardens' Accounts and Court Minute Books of the Goldsmiths' Mistery of London, 1334–1446*, ed. Lisa Jefferson (Woodbridge: Boydell Press, 2003), pp. 196–7 (spelling modernized by LA).

3. *Brut*, p. 339.
4. Christopher Dyer, *Standards of Living in the Later Middle Ages: Social change in England c.1200–1520* (Cambridge: Cambridge University Press, 1989), p. 215 (daily wage), p. 58 (ale), p. 208 (annual rent), p. 75 (monastery school), p. 76 (armour and horses), p. 77 (duke's armour); A. V. B. Norman and Don Pottinger, *English Weapons & Warfare, 449–1660* (London: Arms and Armour Press, 1979), p. 78 (chickens and eggs); A. R. Myers, *London in the Age of Chaucer* (Norman, Okla.: University of Oklahoma Press, 1972), p. 198 (geese), p. 186 (Oxford), p. 53 (fashionable gowns); Douglas Gray, 'Chaucer, Geoffrey (*c*.1340–1400)', *ODNB*.
5. On this stratum of society, see Paul Strohm, *Social Chaucer* (Cambridge, Mass.: Harvard University Press, 1989), pp. 9–13, 22–3.
6. Corpus Christi College, Cambridge MS 61, fol. 1v.
7. California, San Marino, Huntington Library MS Ellesmere 26.C.9, fol. 47r, *Chaucer Multitext* (spelling modernized by LA).
8. On London politics and literature in the 1380s, see Strohm, *Hochon's Arrow*, pp. 11–32, and Marion Turner, *Chaucerian Conflict: Languages of Antagonism in Late Fourteenth-Century London* (Oxford: Clarendon Press, 2007), pp. 8–30.
9. 'Royal sanction of the execution of John Constantyn': 'Memorials: 1384', *Memorials*, pp. 482–3.
10. See Andrew Prescott, 'Brembre, Sir Nicholas (d. 1388)', *ODNB*.
11. *WC*, p. 217.
12. 'Proclamation made in the City, by the King's Command': 'Memorials: 1387', *Memorials*, pp. 490–500 (spelling modernized and some words translated by LA).
13. 'The Appeal and Process' against Brembre and others, section H, article 35: Richard II: Parliament of February 1388, in *PROME*.
14. 'William Hughlot sentenced to lose his hand': 'Memorials: 1387', *Memorials*, pp. 490–500.
15. William Langland, *The Vision of Piers Plowman*, ed. A. V. C. Schmidt (London: Everyman, 1995), Passus I, line 160.
16. *KC*, pp. 499–501.
17. *Concordia*, line 18. On this poem and the broader associations of London with Troy, see Turner, *Chaucerian Conflict*, pp. 56–92.
18. See R. R. Davies, 'Richard II and the Principality of Chester 1397–9', in *The Reign of Richard II: Essays in Honour of May McKisack*, ed. F. R. H. Du Boulay and C. M. Barron (London: Athlone Press, 1971), pp. 256–79.
19. Caroline M. Barron, 'The Quarrel of Richard II with London, 1392–1397', in *The Reign of Richard II*, ed. Du Boulay and Barron, pp. 173–201, at pp. 178–9.
20. *StAC*, I, p. 925.
21. *WC*, p. 496.
22. Nigel Saul, 'Richard II, York, and the Evidence of the King's Itinerary', in *The Age of Richard II*, ed. James L. Gillespie (Stroud: Sutton Publishing, 1997), pp. 71–92, at p. 80.
23. *StAC*, I, pp. 928–31.
24. *WC*, p. 502.
25. See Paul Strohm's chapter 'Queens as Intercessors' in *Hochon's Arrow*, pp. 95–120; and David Wallace, *Chaucerian Polity: Absolutist Lineages and Associational Forms in England and Italy* (Stanford, Calif.: Stanford University Press, 1997), pp. 365–70.

26. *WC*, p. 502.
27. *WC*, pp. 504–6. A Latin praise poem commemorating the event states contrarily that Richard visited St Erkenwald's tomb in St Paul's (*Concordia*, lines 348–9); other chroniclers do not specify.
28. Barron, 'Quarrel of Richard II', p. 194.
29. 'Charge of disloyalty against John Sewale': 'Memorials: 1398', *Memorials*, pp. 546–52.
30. Barron, 'Quarrel of Richard II', p. 180.
31. Ibid., pp. 198–200.
32. *CR*, pp. 132–3.
33. Outbreaks of urban disturbance and violence in York in 1381 were only indirectly connected to the Great Revolt, if at all: see R. B. Dobson, *The Peasants' Revolt of 1381* (London: Macmillan, 1970), pp. 284–9.
34. Dobson, *Peasants' Revolt*, pp. 55, 57.
35. John H. Harvey, 'Richard II and York', in *The Reign of Richard II*, ed. Du Boulay and Barron, pp. 202–17, Appendix, p. 216.
36. For the full list and texts see Richard Beadle, *The York Plays*, 2 vols (Oxford: Early English Text Society, 2009).
37. See Davies, 'Richard II and the Principality of Chester'.
38. Laura Ashe, 'Harold Godwineson', in *Heroes and Anti-Heroes in Medieval Romance*, ed. Neil Cartlidge (Cambridge: D. S. Brewer, 2012), pp. 59–80, at pp. 73–4.

4. SHRINE

1. William Shakespeare, *The Life of King Henry the Fifth*, ed. Claire McEachern, in *Complete Shakespeare*, p. 1151 (IV.i.287–95).
2. The reburial is described and discussed in Paul Strohm, *England's Empty Throne: Usurpation and the Language of Legitimation, 1399–1422* (New Haven, Conn.: Yale University Press, 1998), pp. 115–18.
3. Saul, pp. 428–9.
4. *StAC*, II, p. 151.
5. See Patrick Wormald, 'Earconwald [St Earconwald, Erkenwald] (d. 693)', *ODNB*.
6. See e.g. *Concordia*, lines 347–8. Richard's body was displayed in St Paul's for several days before burial at King's Langley: *StAC*, II, p. 298; *CTM*, p. 103; *Brut*, p. 360.
7. *St Erkenwald*, in *A Book of Middle English*, ed. J. A. Burrow and Thorlac Turville-Petre, 2nd edn (Oxford: Blackwell, 1996), pp. 201–14, lines 321–4 (spelling modernized by LA where possible).
8. *WC*, p. 9.
9. *WC*, p. 11.
10. *WC*, p. 450.
11. Lucy Freeman Sandler, 'The Wilton Diptych and Images of Devotion in Illuminated Manuscripts', in *Regal Image*, pp. 136–54, at p. 154.
12. See Dillian Gordon, 'The Wilton Diptych: An Introduction', in *Regal Image*, pp. 18–26; Nigel Morgan, 'The Signification of the Banner in the Wilton Diptych', in *Regal Image*, pp. 178–88.

13. *StAC*, I, pp. 730–32, 870–74, 882; II, pp. 454, 476–8.
14. *KC*, pp. 260–62, 336; *StAC*, I, pp. 876–8; II, p. 456.
15. *StAC*, II, pp. 56–8.
16. *WC*, p. 42.
17. Saul, pp. 310–11.
18. On the cult of St George, see Andrea Ruddick, *English Identity and Political Culture in the Fourteenth Century* (Cambridge: Cambridge University Press, 2013), pp. 289–94, 300.
19. Usk, p. 65.
20. *StAC*, II, p. 95.
21. *StAC*, II, p. 96.
22. See e.g. *AC*, pp. 123–4.
23. See K. B. McFarlane, *Lancastrian Kings and Lollard Knights* (Oxford: Clarendon Press, 1972), Part Two, pp. 139–226, for the careers of this group.
24. *Twelve Conclusions of the Lollards* (spelling modernized by LA), in *Selections from English Wycliffite Writings*, ed. Anne Hudson (Toronto: University of Toronto Press, 1997), p. 26.
25. See the rebels' letters in *KC*, pp. 222–4.
26. See Anne Hudson, '*Piers Plowman* and the Peasants' Revolt: A Problem Revisited', *Yearbook of Langland Studies*, 8 (1994), pp. 85–106.
27. William Langland, *The Vision of Piers Plowman*, ed. A. V. C. Schmidt (London: Everyman, 1995), Passus XV, lines 552b–66 (spelling modernized by LA).
28. Anne Hudson, 'Wyclif and the English Language', in *Wyclif in His Times*, ed. Anthony Kenny (Oxford: Clarendon Press, 1986), pp. 85–103, at p. 95.
29. Maurice Keen, 'The Influence of Wyclif', in *Wyclif and His Times*, ed. Kenny, pp. 127–45, at p. 131.
30. H. G. Richardson, 'Heresy and the Lay Power under Richard II', *English Historical Review*, 51 (1936), pp. 1–28, at pp. 5–8; Richard II: Parliament of May 1382, item 17, in *PROME*.
31. *KC*, pp. 432–42; *WC*, pp. 318–20, 330.
32. Maureen Jurkowski, 'Latimer, Sir Thomas (1341–1401)', *ODNB*.
33. Richardson, 'Heresy and the Lay Power', p. 19.
34. *StAC*, II, pp. 12–28.
35. Richardson, 'Heresy and the Lay Power', p. 19.
36. Cambridge, Trinity Hall MS 17.
37. Saul, p. 303.
38. Translated in Phillip Lindley, 'Absolutism and Regal Image in Ricardian Sculpture', in *Regal Image*, pp. 60–83, at p. 72.
39. See Charles Kightly, 'Lollard knights (act. *c.*1380–*c.*1414)', *ODNB*.
40. *Twelve Conclusions*, p. 28.
41. Quoted in Saul, p. 301.
42. *KC*, pp. 243–5.
43. Mathew, *The Court of Richard II*, p. 23.
44. I am grateful for the advice of Elizabeth Solopova on this: see her 'Manuscript Evidence for the Patronage, Ownership and Use of the Wycliffite Bible', in *Form and Function in the Late Medieval Bible*, ed. Eyal Poleg and Laura Light (Leiden: Brill, 2013), pp. 333–49; and her forthcoming essay collection, *The Wycliffite Bible: Origin, History and Interpretation* (Leiden: Brill, 2017).
45. See Mary Dove, *The First English Bible: The Text and Context of the Wycliffite Versions* (Cambridge: Cambridge University Press, 2007), pp. 68–82.

46. 'Prologue to Wycliffite Bible, chapter 15', in *Selections from English Wycliffite Writings*, ed. Anne Hudson (Toronto: University of Toronto Press, 1997), pp. 67–8. See Hudson, 'Wyclif and the English Language', pp. 91–2.
47. *Pearl*, in *Poems of the Pearl Manuscript*, ed. Malcolm Andrew and Ronald Waldron (Exeter: University of Exeter Press, 1996), lines 445–52 (spelling modernized by LA).
48. Julian of Norwich, *A Revelation of Love*, ed. Marion Glasscoe (Exeter: University of Exeter Press, 1993), p. 7 (spelling modernized by LA).
49. Saul, p. 321.
50. Saul, p. 313.
51. See e.g. the version of Matthew Paris, *The History of Saint Edward the King*, trans. Thelma S. Fenster and Jocelyn Wogan-Browne (Tempe, Ariz.: Arizona Center for Medieval and Renaissance Studies, 2008), pp. 98–100.

5. EPILOGUE

1. *Richard the Redeless*, lines 23–6.
2. *EngC*, p. 30; cf. *Eulogium*, III, p. 390.
3. *An English Chronicle*, ed. Davies, pp. 24–5 (spelling modernized by LA; reading preferred to *EngC*, pp. 30–31); *Eulogium*, III, pp. 391–2.
4. Henry IV: Parliament of October 1399, item 42, trans. C. Given-Wilson, in *PROME*.
5. *EngC*, p. 23.

Further Reading

By far the best full biography of Richard II is Nigel Saul's magisterial *Richard II* (New Haven, Conn.: Yale University Press, 1997). An earlier biography notable for its psychological reading of Richard is by Anthony Steel (Cambridge: Cambridge University Press, 1941); more recently, Chris Fletcher's *Richard II: Manhood, Youth, and Politics 1377–99* (Oxford: Oxford University Press, 2008) examines the king through the lens of modern gender theory and medieval ideas of masculinity.

The political events and circumstances of the reign are unfolded in several essay collections, most importantly *The Reign of Richard II: Essays in Honour of May McKisack*, edited by F. R. H. Du Boulay and C. M. Barron (London: Athlone Press, 1971), and – including a great deal on Richard's cultural patronage – *Richard II: The Art of Kingship*, edited by Anthony Goodman and James Gillespie (Oxford: Clarendon Press, 1999). On the Wilton Diptych and his other artistic and architectural commissions, see the handsome illustrated volume *The Regal Image of Richard II and the Wilton Diptych*, edited by Dillian Gordon, Lisa Monnas and Caroline Elam (London: Harvey Miller, 1997). Gervase Mathew's *The Court of Richard II* (London: John Murray, 1968) is a slightly old-fashioned but highly readable book. Anthony Tuck has written in powerful detail of the relations between the king and his lords, in *Richard II and the English Nobility* (London: Edward Arnold, 1973). A fascinating, learned and densely written work on late medieval parliaments is Gwilym Dodd's *Justice and Grace* (Oxford: Oxford University Press, 2007), which should ideally be read in combination with J. R. Maddicott's wonderful *The Origins of the English Parliament, 924–1327* (Oxford: Oxford University Press, 2010).

On medieval chroniclers and chronicle-writing Chris Given-Wilson's book is essential: *Chronicles: The Writing of History in Medieval England* (London: Hambledon, 2004). He has also edited and translated the main primary sources for Richard's deposition: *Chronicles of the Revolution, 1397–1400* (Manchester: Manchester University Press, 1993). The St Albans Chronicle is available in translation by James G. Clark as *The Chronica Maiora of Thomas Walsingham, 1376–1422* (Woodbridge: Boydell & Brewer, 2009).

The classic work on chivalry is Maurice Keen, *Chivalry* (New Haven, Conn., and London: Yale University Press, 1984), to which should be added Richard W. Kaeuper, *Holy Warriors: The Religious Ideology of Chivalry* (Philadelphia: University of Pennsylvania Press, 2009), and Craig Taylor, *Chivalry and the Ideals of Knighthood in France During the Hundred Years War* (Cambridge: Cambridge University Press, 2013). The fullest account of England's long war with France is Jonathan Sumption's so far three-volume magnum opus, *The Hundred Years War* (London: Faber & Faber, 1990–2009).

The classic source for the Great Revolt of 1381 is R. B. Dobson, *The Peasants' Revolt of 1381*, 2nd edn (London: Macmillan, 1983). Steven Justice has written an important study of the rebels' communications and their relation to contemporary literature: *Writing and Rebellion: England in 1381* (Berkeley, Calif.: University of California Press, 1994).

A somewhat romanticized sense of daily life in London can be gleaned from A. R. Myers, *London in the Age of Chaucer* (Norman, Okla.: University of Oklahoma Press, 1972). Illuminating on Richard's relationship with Cheshire is Michael Bennett, *Community, Class and Careerism: Cheshire and Lancashire Society in the Age of Sir Gawain and the Green Knight* (Cambridge: Cambridge University Press, 1983), and John M. Bowers, *The Politics of Pearl: Court Poetry in the Reign of Richard II* (Cambridge: D. S. Brewer, 2001);

on Chester's own sense of uniqueness and its expression in literature, see Robert W. Barrett, *Against All England: Regional Identity and Cheshire Writing, 1195–1656* (Notre Dame, Ind.: University of Notre Dame Press, 2009). The mystery pageants are most approachable in *York Mystery Plays: A Selection in Modern Spelling*, edited by Richard Beadle and Pamela M. King (Oxford: Oxford University Press, 2009).

For an accessible overview of medieval society, see *A Social History of England 1200–1500*, edited by Rosemary Horrox and W. Mark Ormrod (Cambridge: Cambridge University Press, 2006); for detailed social and economic history, see the seminal works of Christopher Dyer, *Standards of Living in the Later Middle Ages: Social Change in England c.1200–1520*, rev. edn (Cambridge: Cambridge University Press, 1998), and *An Age of Transition? Economy and Society in England in the later Middle Ages* (Oxford: Clarendon Press, 2005).

Literary scholars have explored the period in provocative depth, using a variety of sources and theoretical approaches. Important works include: Paul Strohm, *Social Chaucer* (Cambridge, Mass.: Harvard University Press, 1989), *Hochon's Arrow: The Social Imagination of Fourteenth-Century Texts* (Princeton, NJ: Princeton University Press, 1992), and *England's Empty Throne: Usurpation and the Language of Legitimation, 1399–1422* (New Haven, Conn.: Yale University Press, 1998); David Wallace, *Chaucerian Polity: Absolutist Lineages and Associational Forms in England and Italy* (Stanford, Calif.: Stanford University Press, 1997); Marion Turner, *Chaucerian Conflict: Languages of Antagonism in Late Fourteenth-Century London* (Oxford: Oxford University Press, 2007).

On Wyclif the most accessible single work is Anthony Kenny's *Wyclif* (Oxford: Oxford University Press, 1985), and there are several important essays in his collection *Wyclif in His Times* (Oxford: Clarendon Press, 1986). The major work on Lollards in politics remains K. B. McFarlane, *Lancastrian Kings and Lollard Knights*

(Oxford: Clarendon Press, 1972). For the whole movement, see Anne Hudson, *The Premature Reformation: Wycliffite Texts and Lollard History* (Oxford: Clarendon Press, 1988), and Lollard writings are helpfully edited in Hudson's *Selections from English Wycliffite Writings* (Toronto: University of Toronto Press, 1997). The Wycliffite Bible is thoroughly contextualized by Mary Dove, *The First English Bible* (Cambridge: Cambridge University Press, 2007).

Robert Bartlett's *Why Can the Dead Do Such Great Things?* (Princeton, NJ: Princeton University Press, 2013) is illuminating on the cult of saints throughout the Middle Ages. On mysticism and visionary writing, *The Cambridge Companion to Medieval English Mysticism*, edited by Vincent Gillespie and Samuel Fanous (Cambridge: Cambridge University Press, 2011), is an excellent guide.

Picture Credits

1. Folio from an illuminated copy of Roger Dymock's anti-Lollard *Treatise Against the Twelve Errors*, *c.*1394–5. Trinity Hall, Cambridge, MS 17, fol. 1r (reproduced by permission of The Master and Fellows of Trinity Hall, Cambridge)
2. Panel of the Wilton Diptych, depicting Richard II with saints, *c.*1395 (National Gallery, London/Bridgeman Images)
3. Panel of the Wilton Diptych depicting the White Hart, *c.*1395 (National Gallery, London/Bridgeman Images)
4. Historiated initial 'N', showing the king, seated with crown, addressing nobles and bishops, from *The Way of Holding Parliament*, English School, *c.*1386–99. British Library, London, Cotton Nero D. VI, fol. 72 (© British Library Board. All Rights Reserved/Bridgeman Images)
5. Interior of Westminster Hall, London (Robert Harding/Alamy)
6. Richard's approach along the Thames to meet the Kentish rebels in 1381. Illumination from Jean Froissart, *Chroniques*, French School, *c.*1470–75 (© Bibliothèque Nationale de France, Paris [MS Français 2644, fol. 154v])
7. Chaucer reading to Richard II. Detail from an illuminated folio of Geoffrey Chaucer, *Troilus and Criseyde*, *c.*1415. Corpus Christi College, Cambridge, MS 61, fol. 1v (reproduced by permission of The Master and Fellows of Corpus Christi College, Cambridge)
8. Radcot Bridge, Oxfordshire (Stephen Oliver/Alamy)
9. The flight of Robert de Vere from Radcot Bridge, 1387. Illumination from Jean Froissart, *Chroniques*, French School,

c.1470–75 (© Bibliothèque Nationale de France, Paris [MS Français 2645, fol. 245v])

10. Wooden funeral effigy head of Anne of Bohemia, 1394 (Westminster Abbey Museum, London/Copyright © The Dean and Chapter of Westminster)
11. Richard receives Isabella of France. Illumination from Froissart, *Chroniques*, French School, fifteenth century. British Library, London, MS Royal 14 D. VI, fol. 268v (© British Library Board. All Rights Reserved/Bridgeman Images)
12. The Dukes of York, Gloucester and Ireland dine with Richard II. Illumination from Jean Wavrin, *Anciennes et nouvelles chroniques d'Angleterre*, French School, *c*.1470–80. British Library, London, MS Royal E. IV, fol. 265v (© British Library Board. All Rights Reserved/Bridgeman Images)
13. Anon., Westminster Abbey portrait of Richard II, English School, 1390s (Westminster Abbey, London/Bridgeman Images)
14. Richard led captive by Bolingbroke to London. Illumination from Jean Creton, *La Prinse et mort du roy Richart*, French School, fifteenth century. British Library, London, MS Harley 1319, fol. 53v (© British Library Board. All Rights Reserved/Bridgeman Images)
15. Mark Rylance as Richard II at the Globe Theatre, London, 2003 (© Tristram Kenton)

Acknowledgements

I am very grateful to Simon Winder for giving me this wonderful commission. Daniel Wakelin read the whole typescript and made numerous helpful comments; Sarah Foot and Stephen Hearn were great interlocutors for my ideas. Finally, I want to thank my father, Philip Ashe, whose lifelong interest in medieval history has always been an inspiration.

Index

Penguin Monarchs

THE HOUSES OF WESSEX AND DENMARK

Athelstan*	Tom Holland
Aethelred the Unready	Richard Abels
Cnut	Ryan Lavelle
Edward the Confessor	

THE HOUSES OF NORMANDY, BLOIS AND ANJOU

William I*	Marc Morris
William II	John Gillingham
Henry I	Edmund King
Stephen	Carl Watkins
Henry II*	Richard Barber
Richard I	Thomas Asbridge
John	Nicholas Vincent

THE HOUSE OF PLANTAGENET

Henry III	Stephen Church
Edward I*	Andy King
Edward II	Christopher Given-Wilson
Edward III*	Jonathan Sumption
Richard II*	Laura Ashe

THE HOUSES OF LANCASTER AND YORK

Henry IV	Catherine Nall
Henry V*	Anne Curry
Henry VI	James Ross
Edward IV	A. J. Pollard
Edward V	Thomas Penn
Richard III	Rosemary Horrox

* Now in paperback

THE HOUSE OF TUDOR

Henry VII	Sean Cunningham
Henry VIII*	John Guy
Edward VI*	Stephen Alford
Mary I*	John Edwards
Elizabeth I	Helen Castor

THE HOUSE OF STUART

James I	Thomas Cogswell
Charles I*	Mark Kishlansky
[Cromwell*	David Horspool]
Charles II*	Clare Jackson
James II	David Womersley
William III & Mary II*	Jonathan Keates
Anne	Richard Hewlings

THE HOUSE OF HANOVER

George I	Tim Blanning
George II	Norman Davies
George III	Amanda Foreman
George IV	Stella Tillyard
William IV	Roger Knight
Victoria*	Jane Ridley

THE HOUSES OF SAXE-COBURG & GOTHA AND WINDSOR

Edward VII*	Richard Davenport-Hines
George V*	David Cannadine
Edward VIII*	Piers Brendon
George VI*	Philip Ziegler
Elizabeth II*	Douglas Hurd

* Now in paperback

ALLEN LANE
an imprint of
PENGUIN BOOKS

Also Published

Jordan B. Peterson, *12 Rules for Life: An Antidote to Chaos*

Bruno Maçães, *The Dawn of Eurasia: On the Trail of the New World Order*

Brock Bastian, *The Other Side of Happiness: Embracing a More Fearless Approach to Living*

Ryan Lavelle, *Cnut: The North Sea King*

Tim Blanning, *George I: The Lucky King*

Thomas Cogswell, *James I: The Phoenix King*

Pete Souza, *Obama, An Intimate Portrait: The Historic Presidency in Photographs*

Robert Dallek, *Franklin D. Roosevelt: A Political Life*

Norman Davies, *Beneath Another Sky: A Global Journey into History*

Ian Black, *Enemies and Neighbours: Arabs and Jews in Palestine and Israel, 1917-2017*

Martin Goodman, *A History of Judaism*

Shami Chakrabarti, *Of Women: In the 21st Century*

Stephen Kotkin, *Stalin, Vol. II: Waiting for Hitler, 1928-1941*

Lindsey Fitzharris, *The Butchering Art: Joseph Lister's Quest to Transform the Grisly World of Victorian Medicine*

Serhii Plokhy, *Lost Kingdom: A History of Russian Nationalism from Ivan the Great to Vladimir Putin*

Mark Mazower, *What You Did Not Tell: A Russian Past and the Journey Home*

Lawrence Freedman, *The Future of War: A History*

Niall Ferguson, *The Square and the Tower: Networks, Hierarchies and the Struggle for Global Power*

Matthew Walker, *Why We Sleep: The New Science of Sleep and Dreams*

Edward O. Wilson, *The Origins of Creativity*

John Bradshaw, *The Animals Among Us: The New Science of Anthropology*

David Cannadine, *Victorious Century: The United Kingdom, 1800-1906*

Leonard Susskind and Art Friedman, *Special Relativity and Classical Field Theory*

Maria Alyokhina, *Riot Days*

Oona A. Hathaway and Scott J. Shapiro, *The Internationalists: And Their Plan to Outlaw War*

Chris Renwick, *Bread for All: The Origins of the Welfare State*

Anne Applebaum, *Red Famine: Stalin's War on Ukraine*

Richard McGregor, *Asia's Reckoning: The Struggle for Global Dominance*

Chris Kraus, *After Kathy Acker: A Biography*

Clair Wills, *Lovers and Strangers: An Immigrant History of Post-War Britain*

Odd Arne Westad, *The Cold War: A World History*

Max Tegmark, *Life 3.0: Being Human in the Age of Artificial Intelligence*

Jonathan Losos, *Improbable Destinies: How Predictable is Evolution?*

Chris D. Thomas, *Inheritors of the Earth: How Nature Is Thriving in an Age of Extinction*

Chris Patten, *First Confession: A Sort of Memoir*

James Delbourgo, *Collecting the World: The Life and Curiosity of Hans Sloane*

Naomi Klein, *No Is Not Enough: Defeating the New Shock Politics*

Ulrich Raulff, *Farewell to the Horse: The Final Century of Our Relationship*

Slavoj Žižek, *The Courage of Hopelessness: Chronicles of a Year of Acting Dangerously*

Patricia Lockwood, *Priestdaddy: A Memoir*

Ian Johnson, *The Souls of China: The Return of Religion After Mao*

Stephen Alford, *London's Triumph: Merchant Adventurers and the Tudor City*

Hugo Mercier and Dan Sperber, *The Enigma of Reason: A New Theory of Human Understanding*

Stuart Hall, *Familiar Stranger: A Life Between Two Islands*

Allen Ginsberg, *The Best Minds of My Generation: A Literary History of the Beats*

Sayeeda Warsi, *The Enemy Within: A Tale of Muslim Britain*

Alexander Betts and Paul Collier, *Refuge: Transforming a Broken Refugee System*

Robert Bickers, *Out of China: How the Chinese Ended the Era of Western Domination*

Erica Benner, *Be Like the Fox: Machiavelli's Lifelong Quest for Freedom*

William D. Cohan, *Why Wall Street Matters*

David Horspool, *Oliver Cromwell: The Protector*

Daniel C. Dennett, *From Bacteria to Bach and Back: The Evolution of Minds*

Derek Thompson, *Hit Makers: How Things Become Popular*

Harriet Harman, *A Woman's Work*

Wendell Berry, *The World-Ending Fire: The Essential Wendell Berry*

Daniel Levin, *Nothing but a Circus: Misadventures among the Powerful*

Stephen Church, *Henry III: A Simple and God-Fearing King*

Pankaj Mishra, *Age of Anger: A History of the Present*

Graeme Wood, *The Way of the Strangers: Encounters with the Islamic State*

Michael Lewis, *The Undoing Project: A Friendship that Changed the World*

John Romer, *A History of Ancient Egypt, Volume 2: From the Great Pyramid to the Fall of the Middle Kingdom*

Andy King, *Edward I: A New King Arthur?*

Thomas L. Friedman, *Thank You for Being Late: An Optimist's Guide to Thriving in the Age of Accelerations*

John Edwards, *Mary I: The Daughter of Time*

Grayson Perry, *The Descent of Man*

Deyan Sudjic, *The Language of Cities*

Norman Ohler, *Blitzed: Drugs in Nazi Germany*

Carlo Rovelli, *Reality Is Not What It Seems: The Journey to Quantum Gravity*

Catherine Merridale, *Lenin on the Train*

Susan Greenfield, *A Day in the Life of the Brain: The Neuroscience of Consciousness from Dawn Till Dusk*

Christopher Given-Wilson, *Edward II: The Terrors of Kingship*

Emma Jane Kirby, *The Optician of Lampedusa*

Minoo Dinshaw, *Outlandish Knight: The Byzantine Life of Steven Runciman*

Candice Millard, *Hero of the Empire: The Making of Winston Churchill*

Christopher de Hamel, *Meetings with Remarkable Manuscripts*

Brian Cox and Jeff Forshaw, *Universal: A Guide to the Cosmos*

Ryan Avent, *The Wealth of Humans: Work and Its Absence in the Twenty-first Century*

Jodie Archer and Matthew L. Jockers, *The Bestseller Code*

Cathy O'Neil, *Weapons of Math Destruction: How Big Data Increases Inequality and Threatens Democracy*

Peter Wadhams, *A Farewell to Ice: A Report from the Arctic*

Richard J. Evans, *The Pursuit of Power: Europe, 1815-1914*

Anthony Gottlieb, *The Dream of Enlightenment: The Rise of Modern Philosophy*

Marc Morris, *William I: England's Conqueror*

Gareth Stedman Jones, *Karl Marx: Greatness and Illusion*

J.C.H. King, *Blood and Land: The Story of Native North America*

Robert Gerwarth, *The Vanquished: Why the First World War Failed to End, 1917-1923*

Joseph Stiglitz, *The Euro: And Its Threat to Europe*

John Bradshaw and Sarah Ellis, *The Trainable Cat: How to Make Life Happier for You and Your Cat*

A J Pollard, *Edward IV: The Summer King*

Erri de Luca, *The Day Before Happiness*

Diarmaid MacCulloch, *All Things Made New: Writings on the Reformation*

Daniel Beer, *The House of the Dead: Siberian Exile Under the Tsars*

Tom Holland, *Athelstan: The Making of England*

Christopher Goscha, *The Penguin History of Modern Vietnam*

Mark Singer, *Trump and Me*

Roger Scruton, *The Ring of Truth: The Wisdom of Wagner's Ring of the Nibelung*

Ruchir Sharma, *The Rise and Fall of Nations: Ten Rules of Change in the Post-Crisis World*

Jonathan Sumption, *Edward III: A Heroic Failure*

Daniel Todman, *Britain's War: Into Battle, 1937-1941*

Dacher Keltner, *The Power Paradox: How We Gain and Lose Influence*

Tom Gash, *Criminal: The Truth About Why People Do Bad Things*

Brendan Simms, *Britain's Europe: A Thousand Years of Conflict and Cooperation*

Slavoj Žižek, *Against the Double Blackmail: Refugees, Terror, and Other Troubles with the Neighbours*

Lynsey Hanley, *Respectable: The Experience of Class*

Piers Brendon, *Edward VIII: The Uncrowned King*

Matthew Desmond, *Evicted: Poverty and Profit in the American City*

T.M. Devine, *Independence or Union: Scotland's Past and Scotland's Present*

Seamus Murphy, *The Republic*

Jerry Brotton, *This Orient Isle: Elizabethan England and the Islamic World*

Srinath Raghavan, *India's War: The Making of Modern South Asia, 1939-1945*

Clare Jackson, *Charles II: The Star King*

Nandan Nilekani and Viral Shah, *Rebooting India: Realizing a Billion Aspirations*

Sunil Khilnani, *Incarnations: India in 50 Lives*

Helen Pearson, *The Life Project: The Extraordinary Story of Our Ordinary Lives*

Ben Ratliff, *Every Song Ever: Twenty Ways to Listen to Music Now*

Richard Davenport-Hines, *Edward VII: The Cosmopolitan King*

Peter H. Wilson, *The Holy Roman Empire: A Thousand Years of Europe's History*

Todd Rose, *The End of Average: How to Succeed in a World that Values Sameness*

Frank Trentmann, *Empire of Things: How We Became a World of Consumers, from the Fifteenth Century to the Twenty-First*

Laura Ashe, *Richard II: A Brittle Glory*

John Donvan and Caren Zucker, *In a Different Key: The Story of Autism*

Jack Shenker, *The Egyptians: A Radical Story*

Tim Judah, *In Wartime: Stories from Ukraine*

Serhii Plokhy, *The Gates of Europe: A History of Ukraine*

Robin Lane Fox, *Augustine: Conversions and Confessions*

Peter Hennessy and James Jinks, *The Silent Deep: The Royal Navy Submarine Service Since 1945*

Sean McMeekin, *The Ottoman Endgame: War, Revolution and the Making of the Modern Middle East, 1908–1923*

Charles Moore, *Margaret Thatcher: The Authorized Biography, Volume Two: Everything She Wants*

Dominic Sandbrook, *The Great British Dream Factory: The Strange History of Our National Imagination*

Larissa MacFarquhar, *Strangers Drowning: Voyages to the Brink of Moral Extremity*

Niall Ferguson, *Kissinger: 1923-1968: The Idealist*

Carlo Rovelli, *Seven Brief Lessons on Physics*

Tim Blanning, *Frederick the Great: King of Prussia*

Ian Kershaw, *To Hell and Back: Europe, 1914–1949*

Pedro Domingos, *The Master Algorithm: How the Quest for the Ultimate Learning Machine Will Remake Our World*

David Wootton, *The Invention of Science: A New History of the Scientific Revolution*

Christopher Tyerman, *How to Plan a Crusade: Reason and Religious War in the Middle Ages*

Andy Beckett, *Promised You A Miracle: UK 80–82*

Carl Watkins, *Stephen: The Reign of Anarchy*

Anne Curry, *Henry V: From Playboy Prince to Warrior King*

John Gillingham, *William II: The Red King*

Roger Knight, *William IV: A King at Sea*

Douglas Hurd, *Elizabeth II: The Steadfast*

Richard Nisbett, *Mindware: Tools for Smart Thinking*

Jochen Bleicken, *Augustus: The Biography*

Paul Mason, *PostCapitalism: A Guide to Our Future*

Frank Wilczek, *A Beautiful Question: Finding Nature's Deep Design*

Roberto Saviano, *Zero Zero Zero*

Owen Hatherley, *Landscapes of Communism: A History Through Buildings*

César Hidalgo, *Why Information Grows: The Evolution of Order, from Atoms to Economies*

Aziz Ansari and Eric Klinenberg, *Modern Romance: An Investigation*

Sudhir Hazareesingh, *How the French Think: An Affectionate Portrait of an Intellectual People*

Steven D. Levitt and Stephen J. Dubner, *When to Rob a Bank: A Rogue Economist's Guide to the World*

Leonard Mlodinow, *The Upright Thinkers: The Human Journey from Living in Trees to Understanding the Cosmos*

Hans Ulrich Obrist, *Lives of the Artists, Lives of the Architects*

Richard H. Thaler, *Misbehaving: The Making of Behavioural Economics*

Sheldon Solomon, Jeff Greenberg and Tom Pyszczynski, *Worm at the Core: On the Role of Death in Life*

Nathaniel Popper, *Digital Gold: The Untold Story of Bitcoin*

Dominic Lieven, *Towards the Flame: Empire, War and the End of Tsarist Russia*

Noel Malcolm, *Agents of Empire: Knights, Corsairs, Jesuits and Spies in the Sixteenth-Century Mediterranean World*

James Rebanks, *The Shepherd's Life: A Tale of the Lake District*

David Brooks, *The Road to Character*

Joseph Stiglitz, *The Great Divide*

Ken Robinson and Lou Aronica, *Creative Schools: Revolutionizing Education from the Ground Up*

Clotaire Rapaille and Andrés Roemer, *Move UP: Why Some Cultures Advances While Others Don't*

Jonathan Keates, *William III and Mary II: Partners in Revolution*

David Womersley, *James II: The Last Catholic King*

Richard Barber, *Henry II: A Prince Among Princes*

Jane Ridley, *Victoria: Queen, Matriarch, Empress*

John Gray, *The Soul of the Marionette: A Short Enquiry into Human Freedom*

Emily Wilson, *Seneca: A Life*